Ogham - Wisdom of the Trees

Jon Dathen

CAPALL BANN PUBLISHING

www.capallbann.co.uk

Ogham - Wisdom of the Trees

©2003 Jon Dathen

ISBN 186163 167 7

Cover design by Paul Mason
All illustrations by Colette Brownrigg colette@riggerjig.u-net.com. Those on pages , by kind permission of Horoscope, the World's Premiere Astrology magazine www.horoscope.co.uk.

Published by:

Capall Bann Publishing
Auton Farm
Milverton
Somerset
TA4 1NE

for

Stuart

Contents

The B-L-N Ogham Stave

B beth SILVER BIRCH	**L** luis ROWAN	**N** nion ASH	**F** fearn ALDER	**S** saille WILLOW
H uath HAWTHORN	**D** duir OAK	**T** tinne HOLLY	**C** coll HAZEL	**Q or CC** quert CRAB APPLE
M muin BLACKBERRY or VINE	**G** gort IVY	**NG** ngetal WHEAT or REED	**Z/SS** straif BLACKTHORN	**R** ruis ELDER
A ailm SCOTS PINE or SILVER FIR	**O** onn GORSE	**U** ur HEATHER	**E** eadha ASPEN	**I** idho YEW

The B-L-N Ogham Stave

6

Introduction

Even today, in Gaelic, the old language of Ireland, the letters of the alphabet are named after trees. This tradition stretches back to a time when an alphabet of 20 nick-like marks, known as ogham, was used for carving on stone monuments. About 375 inscriptions have been discovered. 316 in Ireland, 40 in Wales, 10 on the Isle of Man, a handful in Scotland, and 4 in England. Most date from the 4th century and are in a Celtic language.

Each ogham letter's named after a tree, 'D' is duir (oak), 'T' is tinne (holly) etc. Ogham has an established letter order, and from its first three letters, it's known as the 'Beth-Luis-Nion'.

The ogham alphabet consists of 15 consonants and 5 vowels. The script's written along a central stave which can go up, down or straight along.

Originally it was carved on wood and weapons as well as stone. Tradition preserves that it was used for divination and for explaining the ancient Celtic mysteries. It's sequence of trees forms a sacred calendar, each tree governing a portion of the year.

Although tree ogham's the most widely known, bird ogham, where each letter has a bird name, is just as important.

Ogham's definitely Celtic, but the people we perceive as Celts were an ethnic mix of indigenous tribes, remembered as the 'Old People', descendants of the first nomadic hunters to settle Britain after the Ice Age's end, alongside later incomers; Phoenician and Hebrew traders, refugees from the Trojan war, and tribes from the continent, who blended with the aboriginal population and absorbed their culture.

Julius Caesar stated that, (circa 50BC), most of the tribes in the interior of Britain did not grow corn, but lived on milk and meat and wore skins. His authority has been questioned, but he was no fool, and he was there!

It was these peoples who originated ogham, using it not as an alphabet, but as a memory system, to pass on their knowledge of birds, trees, animals, nature spirits, and their gods.

Their religion had not developed into the pantheism of Greece, Rome or later Celtic Europe, but remained animistic, recognising everything animate and inanimate as spirits, a true faery faith. More powerful deities such as the sun and moon would be appealed to, as would the spirits of animals and trees. The old animistic beliefs were the foundations of all pagan faiths, and have survived in folklore and in the deities of rivers, wells, groves etc, that add so much colour to Celtic, Greek, Roman and Norse mythology.

The druids, a powerful intertribal priesthood, were the lawgivers, scientists and teachers of the ancient Britons. They were religious reformers, who adapted the knowledge of their less organised predecessors, the clan wisemen and women, into a complex theology. They formalised ogham and used it to record their mysteries.

Druidic control was loosened by Rome and smashed by the ascendance of Christianity. Fortunately the druids continued to exist secretly and in changed forms, passing ogham onto their Celtic Christian descendants, and the bards, the wandering poets, historians and genealogists of Wales, ensuring its survival. Once druidism declined, ogham began to be used for secular purposes.

My experience was that there was an alternative stream of tradition, preserved among the naturally conservative population of the English countryside, both as folklore, and more fully as part of the heritage of the Old Religion, the ancient pagan faith preserved from Palaeolithic times. No matter how often rulers or even languages change during history, the people that work on or travel through the land, preserve continuity of culture.

The modern revival of ogham began with a book by the poet and historian Robert Graves. 'The White Goddess' was published in 1948 by Faber & Faber. In it, Graves outlined his theory of poetic inspiration, its links to the ancient Moon-goddess centred religions of Europe, Asia and North Africa, and how these are expressed in tree alphabets such as ogham.

Graves' work is unsurpassed, and while some of his theories cannot now be proven, a correspondent of his informed me that they originated in a reliable oral tradition.

The main argument against Graves is his assertion that the historically extant ogham letter order;
B,L,F,S,N,H,D,T,C,Q,M,G,NG,Z,R,A,O,U,E,I, was not the original.

He gives;
B,L,N,F,S,H,D,T,C,Q,M,G,NG,Z,R,A,O,U,E,I, in which 'N' has been taken from fifth place and restored to third.

Curiously, oral tradition supports Graves fully. He gives as reason for the change, the conquest and take-over of a culturally dominant shrine to Bran, the ancient British god to whom the crow and alder were sacred, by worshippers of the ash god Gwydion. The newcomers, removed 'F', fearn, the alder, from third place where it governed the important spring equinox year phase, 18th March-14th April, when in nature the tree was in first bloom, and substituted 'N', nion, the ash

When much younger I became fascinated by ogham as presented in the pages of the White Goddess. I was attracted to the system's intimate links with nature and the seasons, and felt that it was a vital part of Britain's rich indigenous spiritual heritage. I resolved to discover if this was so by questioning the older people around me who were nurturing my interests in folklore and its associated beliefs.

An old countryman, now long gone, who was well versed in the native mysteries, was puzzled when I questioned him about ogham. He'd never heard of it, but when I explained it as a tree alphabet that formed a seasonal cycle, he exclaimed, "I've not heard of your ogham, but I do know the order of the trees and the birds." He did too, and his 'order' of the trees matched Graves' reconstruction exactly, only muin, the vine became the blackberry, ngetal the reed, became wheat straw, and ailm the silver fir, became the scots pine.

He had no knowledge of any Celtic language, or clue that the trees had the slightest link with any alphabet, but he did know the folklore and symbolism of each one, and how to divine the future with wands cut from them.

It's his knowledge of the trees, birds and divination that will be passed on through these pages.

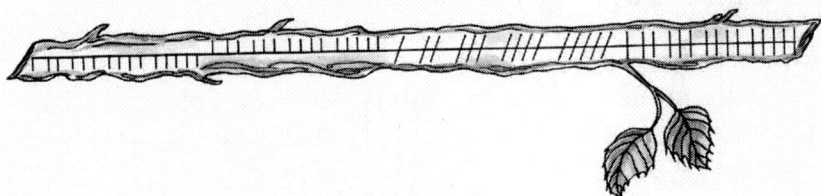

Chapter 1

How to use Ogham

Most people are primarily interested in learning ogham as a fortune telling system and as a key to the ancient British mysteries. It's advisable to learn the Celtic tree names, and which ogham letter relates to which tree, but it is not necessary. It's the order of the trees, their lore and that of the birds associated with them, that's important.

13 ogham trees, birch, rowan, ash, alder, willow, hawthorn, oak, holly, hazel, blackberry, ivy, wheat straw and elder, each emblemise one month of a yearly calendar of thirteen 28 day months. 13 X 28 = 364, leaving one day extra, hence the old saying, 'in a year and a day'. Two trees share months, crab apple lays with hazel, and blackthorn binds with willow. The next five, mark the solstices, equinoxes and the eve of the winter solstice. The scots pine governs the winter solstice, gorse rules the spring equinox, heather the summer solstice, aspen the autumn equinox, while yew has the last day of the solar year, winter solstice eve.

The 21st ogham tree is a tree that is not a tree, the parasitic mistletoe which grows high in the branches of other trees. It has no ogham letter assigned to it, but is considered to be the breath that forms the other letters. Mistletoe rules that 'extra day,' December 23rd, which stands alone between the end of one ogham year, and the start of the next.

To divine with ogham, you need a set of ogham wands, 21 slender but strong branches, cut from the correct tree. If you can't identify the 21 trees, or don't know where to find them, it's an excellent way to learn and connect with the natural world.

The identity of the ogham trees varied according to local availability and differing folk-traditions. In difficulty go to a related species, for instance the grey poplar can stand in for the locally scarce aspen.

There are friendly ways of acquiring wands, without denuding struggling trees and shrubs of valuable limbs. Collect windfall branches after storms, or cut from hedgerows, choosing branches that would be pruned back whenever the hedge's next trimmed. If this isn't possible, cut growth that any good gardener would automatically prune, especially from branches deep within a tree's leaf cover. These interior limbs are in shadow and rarely grow to full potential. Always cut well into the wane of the moon, when the sap's down. Since ogham's based on reverence for tree spirits, it's wise to ask the tree for its branch, explaining what you desire it for. If you're sincere, no ill luck will befall you.

Be careful, as hawthorn, blackthorn and even crab apple thorns can wound, and blackthorn scratches always turn red, sore and irritating.

There's no set length for ogham wands. They should be individual to you, measured from the tip of your middle finger to the inside crease of your elbow. Cut longer in case the wood splits, and then saw to the required length. The width will depend on the tree species, but a slender twig, easy to handle and strong enough to last, is best. Avoid heavy truncheon-like branches. Trim off any foliage, shoots or twigs and sand away rough edges.

Familiarise yourself with your wands as you cut them. Handle them regularly at least until they've thoroughly dried out. If you neglect them and then return months later, many of your dried wands will be unrecognisable, having changed colour and width since you cut them - believe me!

Some people get round this by carving the appropriate ogham character onto each wand, but if you resort to that, perhaps your knowledge of the trees isn't deep enough for you to be using ogham.

Previously, when spiritual knowledge was passed down in strict secrecy, from experienced teacher to trusted pupil, information was given over a far longer time than in today's age of instant 'experts'.

Traditionally, anyone learning ogham was taken to the wood on the 24th December, start of the ogham year, the first day of the birch month, and left to roam until they'd found a suitable tree. After they'd cut a wand, the keys to the folklore and divinatory meaning of the birch and it's bird, the partridge, were given. For the rest of the 27 days of that ogham month, the pupil was left to memorise and meditate on the knowledge that had been granted them. On the 1st day of the next ogham month, its tree was disclosed, a wand cut and its mysteries whispered.

By December 24th of the next year, the secrets of 13 trees and birds had been disclosed. Next, over five months, the 5 solstice and equinox trees were cut, then finally the three vital but hidden trees, blackthorn, crab apple and mistletoe. Sometimes the mistletoe was left until the following December the 23rd, making it two whole years to learn ogham. This method ensures every tree's known before any divination by ogham's attempted.

There are many ways of seeing the truth of a matter with ogham, pick one wand in the morning to clue yourself into the day, or hold a specific question in your mind and select three wands. One to echo the past, one to guide the present, and one to light the future.

For a complete experience, use all twenty-one wands. If you're divining for yourself take them in your hands, meditate or pray, thinking of the time period, day, month or year, which concerns you, and any relevant questions, then cast them onto the table. If you're divining for someone else, they must hold the wands, focus their thoughts and make the cast themselves.

Study the fall of wands, the shapes formed, which are on top, which hidden.Weigh up their meanings and seasonal symbolism. Some will rise to prominence, others recede. Let yourself flow and the wands will inspire you.

Ogham relies on communion with the tree spirits and your own inspirers, rather than a set framework. It can be hard to use effectively but does prove infinitely rewarding.

Please note, neither the author nor the publishers, are responsible in any way, for readers, who while collecting their ogham wands, become lost in forests, fall from trees, or become scratched or otherwise impaled. Please bare in mind that it's unkind to cut branches from immature trees, and that it's often illegal to do so unless you're on your own land - check first! A little common sense will ensure safety and environmental correctness.

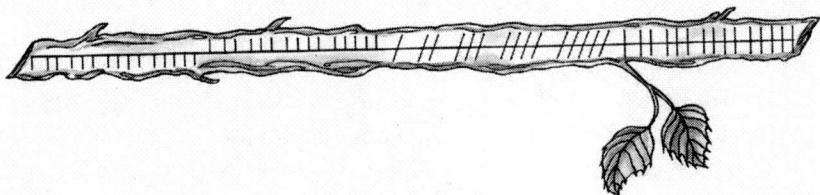

Chapter 2

Birch

Ogham letter: B

The first tree of the ogham cycle is the silver birch (*Betula pendula*), known in Celtic as *beth*. Birch rules the first 28 day month of the ogham calendar, December 24th-January 20th, or if you follow the older purely lunar calendar, the first Moon month of the year, which begins on the first New Moon after the winter solstice.

Enter a birch forest on a night when the moon's more than half full, throwing her light through a clear sky marked with stars, and you'll understand the tree's significance. There's even a smell that goes with a birch grove, an aroma of sap and moss, acidic yet sweet. If the wind blows fresh, then thousands of leaves will rustle, like myriad tinkling voices, and the whole mass of trees will seem to be shaking themselves. In the moonlight the birch trunks glow silver, slender maidenly ghosts floating above the dark ground, like so many white robed priestesses at their devotions. If you're gifted with the 'sight', you may even hear feminine voices from the treetops, chanting together in leafy tones, promising this, prophesying that. The grove has an uncanny feel. You may even sense that you're an intruder, and that if you stay harm will befall you. A crack of a twig underfoot and the wood comes alive, a covey of partridges clatter into the air, short wings whirring, until the birds tumble into a safer roost, clutching at branches in the half light.

To pick a birch wand in divination is fortunate, emblematic of new beginnings and fresh starts. Inspiration for ideas will come and useful plans will form easily. You'll witness your future forming in the actions of others and the situations around you.

It signs that whatever has gone before is truly in the past and has no influence on the present, except as memory and experience. You're able to look forward with clear perceptions, and sense which of your schemes will suit the evolving scene. It's possible that previous situations have ended as part of Fate's plan, to free things for future developments.

Birch signals a time to reassess and lay ghosts to rest, stemming any haunting by regrets, guilt, self-pity, nostalgia, doubts regarding future plans, and lack of self-esteem or confidence.

This phase of genesis is a prime period for communication, both with allies and in prayer, a time to make offerings. Share your aspirations with the spirit realm and promise a sacrifice if they're met - offer time or money to a worthy cause, nature, trees etc.

The silver birch is one of two birch species native to Britain, the downy birch (*Betula pubescens*) is the other. The two are closely related and hybridise regularly. Birches are hardy trees, eagerly colonising recently cleared land and thriving in high mountain air. Apart from the elder it's the first British tree to produce new leaves after winter.

Birch twigs are traditionally cut to make the brush part of old fashioned yard brooms. More painfully they were also used to make the rods with which criminals and lunatics were 'birched', an effective deterrent once current all over Britain. The practice originates in the ancient belief that birch purifies. Malcontents were beaten with it to expel the evil spirits possessing them.

Similarly, birch twigs are used in the old folk ceremony of 'beating the bounds', in which village or town dignitaries lead a procession around the parish boundaries, and various significant landmarks are 'beaten' with the rods. Formerly young boys were birched or thrown into hedges at each stopping place, to indent the memory of the 'bounds'. This ritual drives discontented forces from within the boundaries, renewing the community luck for the year, and when carried out in spring, drives the dark god of winter over the borders. It usually takes place during May, at Rogationtide. This festival begins on Rogation Sunday, which is always 36 days after Easter, itself a movable lunar feast. Rogationtide continues through the Monday, Tuesday and Wednesday. These are known as the 'Gange Days.' The following Thursday is Ascension Day, when the Holy Wells are blessed and dressed.

The witches used birch besoms, to cleanse their household environment spiritually as well as physically. The broom was used for spells of exorcism.

Birch bark is silver white, and in Britain was associated with the White Goddess, the ancient Moon deity, mother of all. She was worshipped under countless names, and like the moon, manifested in three forms that mirror the lifecycle of a woman, New Moon Maiden, Full Moon Mother and Old Moon

Crone. The spirits that ensoul silver birches, partake of the nature of the Maiden and the Crone, which is understandable as the tree governs the end of one year and the birth of another. The Crone's the destroyer, the gatherer, while the Maiden's the force behind the new life germinating within sleeping nature.

The Crone association explains the birch's sometimes sinister reputation as a tree of death. One Somerset birch thicket was haunted by a murderously malevolent female spirit named 'The One with the White Hand'.

Churches were sometimes decorated with birch branches at Whitsun, which falls 10 days after Ascension Day. This remembers the sacred nature of the tree, but was mainly done because the birch's white bark is symbolic of Whitsun, a feast more properly called 'White Sunday'.

Whitsun commemorates Pentecost, when the disciples were inspired by the Holy Spirit. It was named from the white robes of fresh converts, who were traditionally baptised at this time, another association of white with purification and beginning a new life.

The pheasant (*Phasianus colchicus*) is the bird that shares the same ogham letter as the birch. These large game birds are easily visible in the birch month, when the trees have yet to grow their leaves. Although pheasant remains have been found in the debris of excavated Romano-British buildings, they're not native.

The old man who gave me most of my ogham knowledge, said the bird for the birch month was the pheasant or partridge, so the original was probably the partridge (Perdix perdix), an indigenous species, sometimes known mysteriously as the 'bird'.

The partridge's lonely cry summons the vague unease of the birch wood. They're plump, greyish in colour, with an orangey brown face, and are often seen on the ground. The cock carries a chestnut horseshoe marking on his chest, a New Moon with horns down, emblem of the Maiden. The partridge was sacred to love-goddess Venus, one of the Maiden's Roman incarnations, due to its enthusiastic courtship and lovemaking ceremonies.

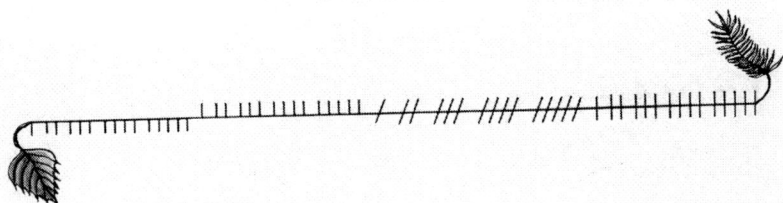

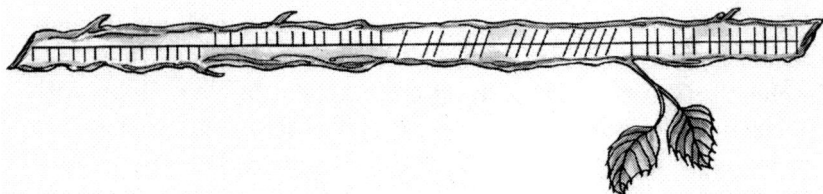

Chapter 3

Rowan

Ogham letter: L

The second tree of the ogham cycle is the rowan (*Sorbus aucuparia*), or in Celtic *'luis'*. The rowan's the tree of the second 28 day month of the ogham calendar, January 21st-February 17th. If you follow the more primitive lunar calendar, rowan rules the second Moon month, beginning on the second New Moon after the winter solstice.

To experience the rowan at her best, climb high above sea level into the hills. Wait for a fine day, when the mountain streams have again begun to run fast, brimming as the first heavy rains of autumn descend to the valleys below in white torrents. The grass is fresh and green, sparkling with dew. Dotted here and there, by streams, overhanging lakes, perched precariously on hillsides, are dainty rowans, full of feminine grace. They give life to the whole scene, as if they're laughing water spirits become trees. Their slender leaves move at one with the wind, cutting the sun's rays into many living shadows. Each bough has clusters of orange berries, and here and there birds flit through the branches, making the most of this annual feast. Where the streams flow into a lake, and the waters become quieter, some mallard ducks are sporting, swimming around calling in their distinctive voices, flicking their wings and tails so that showers of water wet their feathers. A colourful green headed male runs across the water's surface, wings flapping, shooing a rival away from his dowdy brown bride.

To select a rowan wand in divination is a bright sign, promising good fortune, and a secure environment in which to make the most of its blessings. The majority of situations in your life will be flourishing or about to bud with new vigour. It brings a time of opportunity, of quickening, a forwards tide when whatever's begun has a fine chance of growing.

If you are starting a business, new job, study, friendship or anything which will add to your quality of life, it will blossom and eventually yield rewarding fruit. Rowan is particularly fortunate for anything concerning animals, land or beginning a family, as it hints that the fertility spirits of the earth have your welfare at heart. Of course, if you should begin to work against the nature gods, then this would change. Divine blessings bring responsibility.

The Rowan's native to Britain, and is so important in folklore that it's country names are legion. They include; quicken, quickbeam (tree of life), quickerberry, picken, whitten, whitty tree, witchen, and sometimes 'the witch'. Many refer to it as the mountain ash, since it's leaf pattern resembles the larger and sturdier ash tree, and it thrives higher up mountain sides than any other native tree.

Rowan wood's strong and flexible. It was sometimes used for making long-bows, but more commonly for tool handles, poles, barrel hoops, tethering pegs and cradle rockers. Ripe rowan berries can be transformed into a fabulous preserve, rowan jelly, which is eaten with cold game or wild fowl, and is good source of vitamin C. Once the berries are ripe it is a struggle to harvest them before the birds do, as they are loved by all the thrush family and many of the finches.

As witnessed by the tree's names, the rowan's primary folklore associations are with witchcraft and the giving of life. The name 'rowan' is said to derive from the Norse word 'runa' meaning, 'charm', 'secret' or 'spell'. It's the same word as 'rune', the name given to the letters of the Germanic magical alphabet. It is possible that the 'fruit bearing tree', mentioned by Roman author Tacitus, from which the Germanic tribes cut their divinatory rune-slats, was the rowan. They held the tree to be sacred to Thor, the life-bringing thunder-god.

Rowan trees were commonly planted near the house or in the garden to keep dark spirits away and attract fortunate influences. It was considered to be home to the good faeries. Livestock farmers used to cut their whip-stocks from rowan, just as drovers, the men who drove cattle or sheep from farm to farm or market, chose the wood for carving their 'gads', switches used for controlling the animals. These rowan implements also protected the beasts from being overlooked by envious neighbours or other malefic beings. Carters often wore a rowan twig in their hats. Similarly, when oxen ploughed the fields, the pins of their yokes were commonly of rowan.

In many districts rowan crosses were put up in barns on Hallow E'en to ward off unfriendly wandering ghosts and witches, and protect the animals and crops within. A rowan twig bent into a loop and held by a red thread has the same effect, and a piece carried in your pocket ensures safety.

In witchcraft a rowan wand is used for summoning and controlling spirits, and for laying them when they're no longer required. If a rowan sprig's given as a message, it's a sign of affection.

There is an old belief that it's unwise to plant a rowan near an apple tree, as one will kill the other. Whether this is fact or not, it makes symbolic sense. In the ogham cycle, rowan's the gateway of life, the quickening, while the apple is the gateway to the Otherworld, the passage from physical life.

The ancient British associated the tree with the New Moon Maiden incarnation of the White goddess, she of the rowanberry lips.

The bird that shares the rowan's letter and month is the mallard (*Anas platyrhynchos*), otherwise called the mallart or stock duck, Britain's commonest and most popular duck. The dandyish colourful drakes and their drabber brides are a much loved feature of our ponds and parks, where they'll often gather eagerly around anyone who dares to eat a sandwich. In the country they are often warier, as duck makes a tasty dish - try it with rowan jelly!

Mythologically, the duck is sacred to the goddess, because of its abundant fertility. The wife of Odysseus in Homer's Odyssey, is Penelope, which means duck. She was originally a goddess while Odysseus was her sacred king consort.

The duck is an excellent choice of emblem for February, with it's constant rains, high water levels and flooded fields, "Good weather for ducks!"

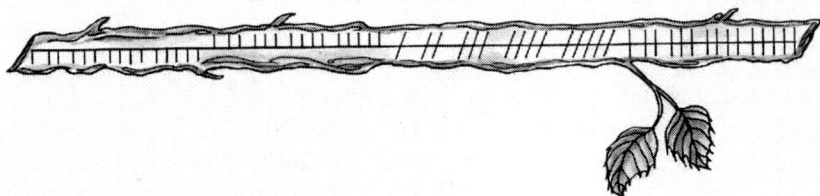

Chapter 4

Ash

Ogham letter: N

The third tree of the ogham cycle is the common ash (*Fraxinus excelsior*), or in Celtic, *nion*. The ash governs the third 28 day month of the ogham calendar, February 18th–March 17th, or in the older lunar calendar, the third Moon month, which begins on the third New Moon after the winter solstice.

To enter the secret world of the ash, choose a late summer day, and delve into an ancient grove, that shares a deserted valley with a narrow faery haunted stream. The moss underfoot is sticky with last years fallen ash keys, the air moist with water vapour. The silver grey trees stretch a hundred feet up into the crystal sky, impressing with their androgynous strength. On slender branches, thousands of ash leaves, arrayed in orderly rows like warriors, rustle ancient songs, and through them the amber sunlight beams, are urged to dance by the wind in swirling harlequin patterns.

Choose one tree, and feel its smooth trunk with the palm of your hand. The wood feels cold, in some places there's velvety moss, but above all there's a presence of dependable strength, of a being, stately and enduring. Not far away, the mud flats at the edge of a lake, provide a meeting place for families of snipe. The little brown birds wade about among the reeds, like stilt-legged inspectors, searching the mud with their long thin bills. From a distance they've white stripes running the length of their backs. Occasionally one becomes disturbed and takes to the air with a jarring cry, spreading alarm through his tiny flock.

To draw the ash wand during divination is a relief. It signs that whatever your troubles, the gods are casting a favourable eye on you, lending support and assistance. A friend or ally will come forward to aid and guide you, or situations arise that will turn events in your favour. If things are out of your control, you'll regain command. It summons the moral or physical support of another person, situation or institution. Although you'll be aided, do be sure to keep striving yourself. It's an old saying that, 'The gods help those who help themselves'.

If you're planning a new venture, you'll attract the backing you need. Resources, mental and physical will be supplied. If you're unwell, a healing process will begin.

The ash wand can predict a meeting with someone who'll become that rarity - a real friend!

Ash is one of Britain's best loved trees. Its strong and flexible white wood is made into oars, spars, hoops, hurdles, coach shafts, tool handles, bows and spear shafts.

The ash is regarded as man's helper and ally. Most of its folklore reflects it's status as the tree of Odin, the chief Germanic god. Most European peoples were of mixed but common descent, and their myths, deities and rites were mainly variations on a theme. Celtic tribes had an ash god named Gwydion, who is identified with Odin. It was he who become supreme in pre-Roman Britain, replacing the ancient British alder god Bran.

Some tribes placed the ash god as their chief deity, recognising their sacred king as his earthly incarnation. One of his duties was to make rain, and for this he used ash sprigs. Primeval legend tells of a time before agriculture, when the samara, the seed bearing ash keys, were consumed as a staple part of daily diet. Even recently they were preserved in salt and vinegar and eaten as a pickle.

Old countrymen would carve their whipstocks from ash, as the wood protected their animals from malefic magic and gave them better control. This comes from the association of the ash with horses. The Norse Odin and the Greek Poseidon, both ash gods, had the horse as their sacred animal and were responsible for the fertility of the herds, and the mysteries of horse training. In myth, Poseidon made love to the harvest mother Demeter, while both wore horse form. Their cult's reflected in ancient Britain by that of Epona, the mare and harvest goddess. The ancient Greeks named the ash nymphs, the feminine souls of the trees, meliae.

An ash stick was considered the best weapon against snakes, and in West Somerset, a wreath of flowers was hung on the ash nearest a farm, as an offering to garner the tree's protection against serpents, for both humans and animals.

Ash trees had healing powers too. For every wart on a person cut a notch in an ash wand, and then throw it over your right shoulder. Sickly children can be enlivened by passing them through a gap in the trunk of an old split ash tree, and to cure farm animals of the quarter ail, sacrifice a shrew and seal it within a natural hole in a living ash. These cures remember the ash as the Tree of Life, in whose branches all creation flowered. The tree has a special resonance with mankind, since it was from ash wood that the gods carved the first man.

In any year in which no keys grew on the ash trees, a public calamity is prophesied.

The snipe (*Gallinago gallinago*) is a small wading bird with an incredibly long bill, useful when probing for insects. It haunts mudflats and marshes. Country names include; air goat and heather bleater.

The snipe, like the ash, is associated with thunder and rain, because of the thunder-like sound it drums up during it's courtship display. The males rise high in the air and then dive quickly, making a rhythmic noise like a goat bleating, by vibrating their wings and tail. The Faroe islanders see this performance as an omen of rain, or snow if it's heard on March 25th. It could be that unusual weather's predicted if the snipe's heard outside it's own ogham month, which ends March 17th.

Through Latvia and Germany it's believed to be a thunderbird, responsible for bringing storms or predicting them. The Latvians name the bird, thunder's she-goat, or he-goat. The Germans call it the weather-bird, storm-bird or rain-bird. As a weather prophet the snipe is man's ally, and it's association with thunder, connects it with rainmaking and the wet late February, early March, time period.

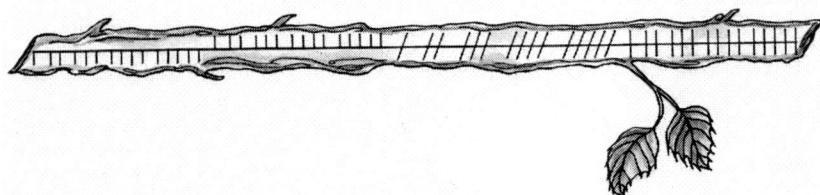

Chapter 5

Alder

Ogham letter: F

The alder (*Alnus glutinosa*), or in Celtic *fearn*, is the fourth tree of the ogham cycle. In the ogham calendar it governs the fourth 28 day month, March 18th-April 14th, or if you prefer the older lunar calendar, the fourth Moon month, which begins on the fourth New Moon after the winter solstice.

To understand the alder, travel into its own land, a hidden valley of lush grass, moss and mists, where gurgling swift streams run through deep ancient channels. The alders have grown large, rivalling oaks in size. Some are gathered in groups overhanging the racing waters, their roots visible in the water, while larger trees stand alone. There's a distinctive smell, pleasant, woody, touched by a note of decay. The alder leaves cut down the light, darkening the air, and the trees seem to watch and wait, emanating a feeling that you'd better be gone before dark, their silence hinting at forbidden secrets. Beyond the forest edges where the streams run into farmland, a team of oxen are ploughing, steadily turning the rich brown soil. The air's filled with the raucous cries of gulls, as they dive and swirl, jostling for a chance to pick at the worms and insects left exposed on the fresh turned earth. The gulls are white against the furrows, concentrated points of light, pure and undefiled. Follow the streams down to the coast, and there are other gulls reaping the sea's harvest, some standing on the sand, a few wheeling in the air, more bobbing on the waves far out to sea.

To pick an alder wand when divining gives cause for thought. It signs that change is inevitable, Fated to occur. It leaves a bittersweet taste, something must be sacrificed, a love, career, friend, hobby, a project or possession. Whatever it may be, it's time is up and something fresh will grow in its place. You may feel sadness, but you'll see the reason in due course, once the time of change has passed. Rest assured that the transform-ations the alder brings are a necessary cleansing. It's better to accept this and be flexible, than go through the terrible fire of vainly hanging on to what must fade.

The alder wand makes us aware of the sadness of the gift of prophecy, a sense of the inevitability of all things.

The alder, called the 'aul' in Herefordshire, has rather a gloomy reputation. When the wood's cut it bleeds, taking on a ruddy orange colour. It's a tree of wetlands, and its root systems strengthen the banks of stream and river banks, preventing erosion. It's an agent of transformation as its roots extract nitrogen from the air. Making up for that element's low availability in wet soil. This enriches the surrounding earth. The leaves are shield shaped and the fruits resemble small black pine cones.

Alder wood's water resistant and was used as piles, pointed stakes driven into river beds as support for bridges or houses. Venice once rested on alder piles. The wood's used for furniture making in the Scottish Highlands, where it's known as Scottish mahogany and elsewhere for cartwheels, spinning wheels, clogs, spoons, and numerous other implements. The alder's most famous for the dye its bark produces, a fine red colour (Aldine Red). The young shoots dye yellow, the fresh wood dyes pinkish fawn, and the catkins give green.

Alder's perhaps the earliest sacred tree. Primitive European houses were built on alder piles, and its red dye was used to stain the face of the sacred king, the magician ruler believed to be the human embodiment of the alder god. This deity, consort of the Moon and harvest goddess, developed many names and forms across Europe and Asia, and was the masculine godhead of the earliest religious system. Primarily a corn god, he was born in the spring, and sacrificed at the harvest, when his spirit would take up residence in the alder groves.

The alder god's earthly representative was originally sacrificed by beheading at the end of his one year reign, when a new king was elected. The dead king's corpse was eaten as a communal meal, and his head embalmed to serve as an oracle. This was probably done by placing alder pipes around it, to bleat as the winds blew through the alder holt in which it was preserved. This ghostly piping would've then been interpreted by his priests or priestesses.

The ancient British name of this god was Bran, and remnants of his legend, including his beheading, are preserved in the Welsh Mabinogion. Although this collection of Celtic folktale and legend dates from the 13th century, it contains very early material. Bran's sacred bird was the prophetic crow, still widely considered to be the 'Devil's bird'. In Phrygia he was Sabazius, in Rome, Saturn, and in Greece, Cronus. Although some authorities claim Cronus means 'time', it originally meant 'crow'.

In folklore the alder was believed to be home to a malignant spirit, and it was thought unlucky to meddle with the trees, as if the ghost of the sacred king haunted them. "If you wander into an alder holt alone, you may never be seen again, as they'll keep 'ee."

The woody catkins are known as black knobs, and in Derbyshire they're used as decorations for well dressing. This makes an interesting link between the alder and sacred wells.

The herring gull (*Larus argentatus*) is emblematic of British seaside resorts, with it's yellow bill and legs, white and grey plumage, unmistakable cry and cheeky behaviour. They're Britain's commonest gull and can live for 30 years. Their success as a species is a tribute to their adaptability and intelligence. They eat almost anything, from fish, to carrion, to chips.

The gull is a fitting bird to share the alder's ogham month. An old birdkeeper once confided, "Gulls and crows, there's no difference, only that the gulls love the sea more. They even speak the same language." Gulls, like the alder, bridge the gap between the water and the land, being equally at home in both environments

There's an old belief, once common along Britain's coasts, that gulls are enspirited by the souls of old sailors. This mirrors the Somerset and Cornwall myth, that the soul of Arthur, another slain sacred king, flies as a raven or chough.

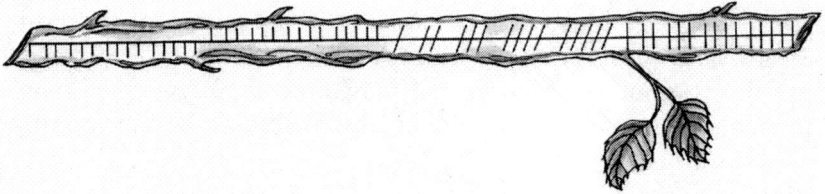

Chapter 6

Willow

Ogham letter: S

The white willow (*Salix alba*) is the fifth tree of the ogham cycle. In the ogham calendar it rules the fifth 28 day month, April 15th-May 12th, or if you prefer the older lunar calendar, the fifth Moon month, which begins at the fifth New Moon after the winter solstice.

To see willows in their true light, choose a midsummer night, when the moon is full. Wade through a thick meadow in southern Britain, down to where a deep, dark river, flows silently and strongly. You can smell the water before you reach it. It's algae moist scent mingles with that of the sleeping flowers and bruised grass. Leaning out across the waters, immense willows tower, drooping their slender branches almost into the torrent. Silver moon white dances from the reflective underside of their spear pointed leaves, accentuating their dense moving shadows. Feel the bark that protects the wide trunks. Your fingers can disappear in its black valleys and rough chasms. In the slightest breeze` the willows whisper, communing, knowing. Their presences surround you, and it seems occasionally as if one's moved to stand behind you, to listen more intently to your thoughts. To escape your mind invokes another scene, a memory of the day's bright sunlight, a cliff by the sea, and a flash of light as a large bird passes. As it flies, it's head turns. You mark the long pointed wings, curved beak, and yellow legs of a peregrine falcon, and then it's gone. Later you see it high above a field. Suddenly, it's wings fold, it arrows from the sky and disappears, dropping towards its unsuspecting quarry.

If you select a willow wand in divination it whispers a secret and sheds a tear. It omens grief, rejection or unrequited love, advising realism concerning any current attachments. There will be a parting, a split from a lover, or emotional betrayal. The willow instills awareness of reality, a glimpse into the true nature of life and Fate, a realisation of the world's sadness.

It reassures, that whatever has caused your sorrow, was an enchantment, something neither real in a true sense, nor ever destined to last. However, emotions disobey logic. You can still mourn an illusion.

The insight this tree grants into the future, gives time to prepare. Winnowing fans were made of willow. In the days when wheat was harvested by hand, these were used to create a draught, to separate the wheat from the chaff - the usable grain from the debris. The life-experiences brought by the willow are the tests which force us to grow. They divide the strong from the weak.

The willow is a prophetic tree, and reflects in its visions, the changeability of its mistress, the moon, who's transformations promote the sobering fact, that everything that exists must eventually change its form. All things are part of an enchantment, a glamour that hides a greater truth. The reality we exist in, from the perspective of a tree, is as fleeting as a summer breeze.

The willow is still a feature of landscapes such as the Somerset levels, where they line the rivers, streams and rhines, that drain the low lying fields. Despite the tree's magical reputation, it's proved useful to man. The willow's sturdy roots bind the riverbanks, preventing erosion. They were once planted for this purpose, and pollarded to provide wood.

To pollard a tree, it's top is regularly cut off at head height. The new growth provides a crop of poles, used for fencing, basketry and firewood. The willow family's ancient, and includes the weeping willow, crack willow and osier.

Some claim the osier (*Salix vimnalis*) to be the ogham's willow. The osier is a shrub, and is coppiced, cut down to ground level every year, to produce 'withies,' pliant stems for basketry, fish traps, chair and cradle making. The willows flower through April and May, their own ogham month.

Of all the trees, the willow's said to love the water most, and is therefore sacred to the Moon goddess, mistress of the world's rivers, streams and oceans. In folklore, the tree's associated with her magical arts, enchantment and divination, and so has a sinister witch-like reputation.

It was considered foolish to linger too long on a lonely road girded by willows, for, as the old rhyme suggests, "Willows do walk." They were thought to follow unwary travellers, muttering to themselves. A sprig of willow was the sign for someone rejected in love.

The bird that shares the fifth ogham month is the peregrine

falcon (*Falco peregrinus*). This spectacular bird of prey is both beautiful and deadly. It symbolises the glamour and savagery of love and life. An unfortunate tribute to its prowess as a hunter, was its near extinction at the hands of gamekeepers, intent on preserving their pheasants and grouse. Luckily, government intervention and increasingly relaxed attitudes have ensured its survival.

Frequently to be seen near their nest sites on coastal cliffs, peregrines prey mostly on other birds. By folding their wings and stooping at their quarry from above, they can achieve a speed of 180 mph. Peregrines are revered by falconers for providing the most exciting sport, especially the females, who're bigger and more aggressive. Their reputation as royal birds, reminds that many English monarchs were keen falconers, who always favoured the peregrine.

The Irish source for bird-ogham, the mediaeval *Book of Ballymote*, gives 'hawk' as the bird of the fifth month. The peregrine's taxonomically classified as a falcon, rather than a true hawk such as the goshawk. However, poets and mythographers are rarely biologists, and just over a hundred years ago, the sporting writer Stonehenge, in his *British Rural Sports* (G. Routledge & Co. 1857), still described goshawks and sparrowhawks as 'short winged hawks,' and the peregrine and kestrel as 'long winged hawks.'

While the willow is a tree of the moon, the peregrine is sacred to the sun. The Egyptian sun gods Ra and Horus, had falcon forms and were depicted with falcons' heads. In Horus' case, the bird was envisaged as the sky, the sun one eye, and the moon the other.

Arthur's knight Gawain, began his legendary career as the Welsh hero Gwalchmei, the 'Hawk of May.' What better name for a falcon headed sun god, whose sacred bird rules the fifth month?

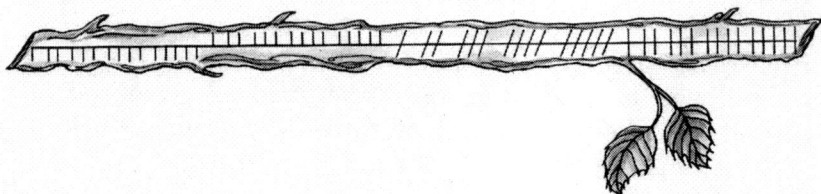

Chapter 7

Blackthorn

Ogham letter: Z / SS

The blackthorn (*Prunus spinosa*), in Celtic *straif*, shares the place of *saille*, the willow, in the ogham cycle. So it jointly governs the fifth 28 day month, April 15th-May12th, or in the older purely lunar calendar, the fifth Moon month, which begins at the fifth New Moon after the winter solstice.

This month sharing is for mythological as well as alphabetic reasons. Blackthorn's ogham letter, 'Z', was once written 'SS', similar to willow, ogham's 'S'. Blackthorn's the badge of the crone incarnation of the Moon goddess, the winter queen. Placed during the month that contains May Day, start of the summer half of the year, it reminds that winter waits within summer. The apple tree, emblem of summer's bounty, sacred to the fertile Full Moon Mother, shares the ninth month, August 5th-September 1st, with hazel, marking the start of the harvest season, prelude to winter.

To discover the blackthorn's ways, it is best to walk one of Britain's ancient trackways in early April, a narrow rough footpath, bounded on one side by meadow, on the other by carefully preserved hedgerow. At the hedge's base there's cleavers and nettles. Everywhere bramble curves, baring its thorns and flaunting its delicate flowers. There are elms and hazel, here and there a wild rose or crab apple. All branches and stems are bound together, by growth and the hand of a skilled hedger, forming a living impenetrable wall.

Further down there are clouds of white blossom. Draw nearer and you know instinctively you're in the presence of blackthorns. Peer into the hedge and you're within a tangled thicket, a dark dense mass of wood, with innumerable branches and twigs, all armed with piercing thorns. No one passes through a blackthorn hedge. The five petalled flowers are enchanting, yet the trees emanate a formidable spirit, more indomitable than the elms surrounding them. Surprisingly there are small tits and finches hopping around within the blackthorn, safe in its protection. A burst of song draws your eye upwards, and for a second you see a speckled song thrush outlined against the sky, throat puffed out in song. Then its gone, with a flutter of wings and a harsh call of annoyance, "Tchuck, tchuck, tchuck!"

Choose a blackthorn wand when divining and you know there is stormy weather ahead. It signs the need to be strong and resolute, to meet head on the challenges that will be put before you. There will be conflict and inhospitable conditions. Opponents to your schemes or beliefs will emerge, and will need to be dealt with.

Blackthorn never advises compromise or retreat. Its message is of realising your responsibilities to yourself, your family, social grouping or nation, and fighting for their rights. Strife will force you to take command, or cause authority to be granted you. So out of difficulty, promotion could be won. At the least, your inherent leadership capabilities will come to the fore.

Spiritually it reminds of the need to take absolute responsibility for your own actions and accept their consequences. This is the true meaning of the word 'karma'.

If you believe in such things, the blackthorn wand was thought to omen that an ill wish or curse had been placed on you. It can reveal reproductive troubles or a mishap during pregnancy.

The blackthorn is a large shrub or small tree, probably the ancestor of our domestic plum trees. They are an integral part of the British countryside, whether planted in hedgerows, or occurring wild in woodland. The wood is extremely hard and is used for walking sticks, cudgels and the teeth of hay rakes. The tree's bitter purple-black fruits are known as sloes. They can be made into jam or wine, but sloe gin is more popular. Sloes and sugar are packed into a half-full bottle of gin. Over a year and a day, it ferments and produces a blood red liquor, a nip of which keeps out the severest cold. In Plymouth, Devon, sloes are known as bullums.

In folklore the blackthorn is a tree of witchcraft. Country people avoid them, regarding them as unlucky, or the property of the Devil. Witches traditionally carry blackthorn walking sticks, 'black rods', which when pointed at an intended victim, can be used as 'blasting sticks', to lay curses.

The tradition that a blackthorn stick is a badge of authority or supernatural power, can be witnessed in parliamentary custom. When the MPs in the House of Commons are officially called to the House of Lords, it is the monarch's official messenger, the Gentleman Usher of the Black Rod, or plain 'Black Rod' that summons them.

If blackthorn wood is brought into a house it will cause a death or bring news of one. A 'blackthorn winter' occurs if it is gloomy and bitingly cold, with a harrowing north-east wind, when the blackthorns are in bloom. This omens a spoiled summer and harsh winter. It is unwise to plant anything tender until a blackthorn winter is over, but it is lucky to sow barley while the trees are in flower.

The song thrush (*Turdus philomelos*), whose country names include, mavis, throstler and whistling dick, is the bird associated with the blackthorn's ogham month. This much loved garden bird has suffered decline as the result of changed farming methods, but luckily it's still fairly common. Visually it is best identified by it's white breast and face, speckled with dark brown spots. It's crown, neck, back and tail are olive-brown.

The tone and vibrancy of the thrush's song is spectacular. Every bird's song is unique, and over a period of time they improvise and add to their personal symphony, sometimes including novelty phrases, such as an impression of a car alarm. Interestingly, it is noticeable that some individuals are more creatively inspired than others.

Thrushes are beautiful, but as any gardener will confide, they are avid hunters of worms, insects and snails. They often select a favourite stone for a dining table, and bash snails to pieces on it.

The Romans fattened thrushes for the table in their thousands. They're still eaten in southern Europe, and are hunted when the sloes are harvested, by which time the birds have taken advantage of the ripe grapes and olives, and are at their heaviest. A French proverb says, 'As drunk as a thrush.' This comes from the belief that the birds gorge on fermenting grapes and become tipsy.

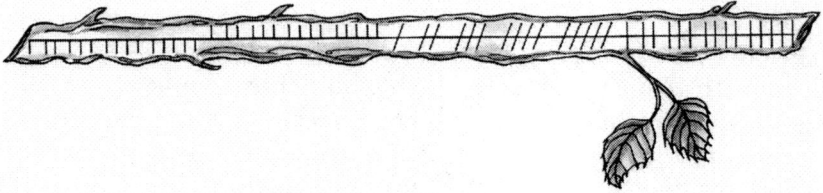

Chapter 8

Hawthorn

Ogham letter: H

The hawthorn (*Crataegus monogyna*), in the Celtic tongue *uath*, takes sixth place in the ogham cycle. In the ogham calendar it governs the sixth 28 day month, May 13th - June 9th, or if you keep time by the old lunar calendar, the sixth Moon month, which starts at the sixth New Moon after the winter solstice.

To witness the magic of hawthorn, search for them on or around the 11th of May. A pasture in Somerset's ideal, where rich red Devon cattle chew the thick grass, and the sunlight's angle speaks of late afternoon. Things seem vivid, shimmering, the grass greener than usual. The hedges round the field are hawthorn, kept low and bushy by the hedger's skill. Three hawthorns at the field's centre have been allowed to grow into trees. They inhabit a craggy grass mound, too steep to plough. Their glossy leaves are vivid green, and they're clouded by pink and white blossom, fragrant with musky scent. From nearby comes the harsh call of a raven. He's standing on a tree stump, throat puffed out as he caws. Four times he calls, bowing each time. His display finished, he rises into the air with a sweep of broad black wings, flight feathers outstretched like fingers.

If you're fortunate enough to draw a hawthorn wand during divination, expect a touch of magic to enchant your life. This could be anything from a magical event, or a feeling of deja vu, to a stroke of luck, a helping hand from the spirit world. It could be a renewed sense of wellbeing, or healing after illness.

While you're under the spell of the hawthorn it's as well not to enter on any new love relationships or marriages, or be profligate in any way, whether by boasting of good fortune or ostentatiously displaying wealth. It warns not to dissipate energies, to be controlled and focus on treading the life-path you've set yourself.

The hawthorn, known as whitethorn, maythorn or quickthorn, is common throughout Britain's countryside, growing both wild and purposefully planted for hedging. Its thorns and dense sturdy growth means that when laid as a hedge, it forms a formidable living barrier. The hawthorn's scarlet fruits, haws, are loved by birds such as fieldfares and hawfinches, and can be made into a tasty jelly or country wine. They're rich in vitamin C.

In Britain, country people regard the hawthorn with respect. It was the property of the faeries, and often marked the entrance to their world. A hawthorn wand was used for casting spells. It was unlucky to chop the tree down or bring cuttings into the house. Anyone foolish enough to do so risked invoking illness and death. On one day of the year this was relaxed. This was May Day, May 1st, or in the unreformed calendar Old May Day, May 11th, the ancient feast of summer's start, preserved in Celtic folklore as Beltane.

If a flowering bough was brought in on this day, it radiated luck, and any woman who washed her face in dew collected from hawthorn trees, would stay forever young.

May Day was a special time, when nature elementals, faery folk and the spirits of the departed were out and about, and easily contacted. British folk celebrations were plentiful at this time, mostly consisting of 'bringing in the may,' where youngsters would merrily disappear into the woods together to collect hawthorn boughs. There'd be village processions and dances later. Likewise, the faeries and other spirits were believed to hold their own feasts and processions.

If anyone built their house of hawthorn wood, severe misfortune would curse those within. Hawthorn trees were believed to love cattle, and stock grazed in a field where they grew always flourished. If a cynical farmer ploughed the trees up to make more room, all the goodness would leave the land.

The Romans purified their temples and hearths during May, and abstained from sex, marriage, cutting their hair or wearing new clothes. This was probably because the hawthorn month was originally sacred to the gods, faeries and the ancestors, and to do anything worldly during it was taboo.

In the mediaeval Irish sources, the bird that shares the sixth ogham month, is the night-crow. This name is found in other contemporary manuscripts and legends, which proves a particular bird was referred to. Of course, none of the corvids, birds of the crow family, fly at night, so the night-crow is either a creature of folklore or a nickname for a nocturnal species. Various birds have been put forward as candidates, including the tawny owl, nightjar, bittern and cormorant.

The answer lies in the myth of the Wild Hunt, the ghostly procession of spirits, faeries, spectral hounds and witches, which is believed to hunt the night sky, scenting out souls ripe for harvest. This troupe is led by the local god of the dead, whether Herne the Hunter, King Arthur, Bran or Odin. In Denmark the outrider for the Wild Hunt was the night-raven. Both Bran and Odin are associated with ravens, and it was the cry of this bird, heard at night, which was believed to presage a passing to the Otherworld.

So the night-crow is not the raven as a species, but a particular supernatural raven, who's the bird of the Otherworld god, leader of the wild hunt, Lord of the dead. The boundary between an animal or bird being the familiar or totem of a deity and being the god himself is blurred. If ancient Egypt is typical, the gods were animals, birds, even insects, before they gained their human forms. This is remembered in the beliefs of many tribal peoples, who see the creatures around them as messengers of the gods, or the gods themselves. All beings are spirits, a god or goddess is a particularly powerful spirit, and all spirits are part of the Great Spirit.

The raven of day (*Corvus corax*) has long been associated with witchcraft, due to its supreme intelligence, legendary longevity and ability to mimic man when in captivity. It's unflagging loyalty to one owner made it the ultimate witch's familiar, and as the totem of the witches' god, Bran or Herne, it came to embody psychic powers and communication with the shades of the departed.

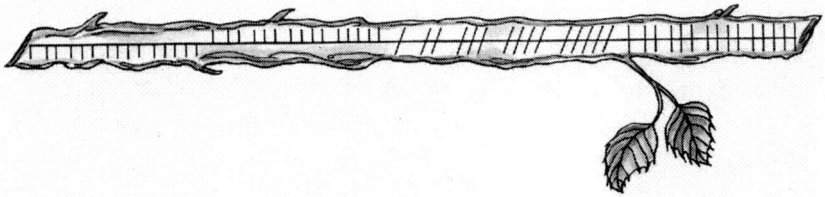

Chapter 9

Oak

Ogham letter: D

The English oak (*Quercus robur*), or in Celtic *duir*, has seventh place in the ogham cycle. In the ogham calendar it rules the seventh 28 day month, June 10th - July 7th, or if you prefer the ancient lunar calendar, the seventh Moon month, beginning at the seventh New Moon after the winter solstice.

To witness the majesty of oaks, enter an ancient forest in autumn. It is soft underfoot, with countless fallen leaves heaped over a deep moss carpet. Oaks of enormous girth and height tower all around, each a silent terrific presence. Some have been standing for hundreds of years, their fissured trunks thirty feet wide, their uppermost branches rearing a hundred feet into the air, resembling the antlers of gigantic stags. Their lower branches reach like extended arms, thirty feet in each direction. Acorns are strewn everywhere. Stop and listen and the silence is filled, first with the rustle of millions of dried golden leaves, then with the buzzing of thousands of insects, and the song of hundreds of birds - the forest is alive. From a low branch a tiny brown bird hops, a wren, so quick and small you wonder if it's real. Its short stumpy tail wags up and down. It catches sight of you and flies out of sight among the leaves, scolding heartily.

If you're fortunate enough to choose an oak wand during divination, you can feel safe, protected. It signs that whatever life brings, you have the strength and endurance to see things through, to survive and prosper. It symbolises continuation and tradition, making a stand to preserve what you hold dear, whether belief, family, nature or nation. When in doubt about a course of action, an oak wand advises that you should be firm and unyielding. It can be a sign of the need to protect others.

If you've been going through changes or a period of insecurity, it signals that you'll be sheltered, and that security will return, provided you stay on course. The gods are on your side and will see justice done, sometimes granting you the opportunity for revenge.

Oaks have always been considered royal trees, in former times for religious reasons, more recently because Queen Elizabeth I, reserved them for the construction of her navy's ships. Oak wood is tough and durable, and is prized by cabinet makers and builders of traditional cottages. Most of the blackened beams in British buildings are oak. The tree's bark was used to tan leather and to produce a purple dye. Acorns, the fruit of the oak, provide valuable fodder for pigs, and some peoples still bake bread with acorn kernel flower.

In pre-agricultural times acorns were a valuable addition to diet. They taste better if they're dried! In many cultures the oak was sacred, and associated with the king of the gods;

Jupiter in Rome, Zeus in Greece, and Thor in Norway. Although some ancient peoples of Britain made their principal male deity an alder or ash god, the oak-king was represented here too, as witnessed by Herne the Hunter, the antlered ghost who haunts Windsor Great Park. He's a memory the stag and oak god of the Old Religion.

The oak month, the seventh, contains the summer solstice. Solstice Eve, Midsummer Night, was an important festival across Europe. In Britain, it was a faery feast, when bonfires would burn on every hilltop. Sometimes images of a god were burnt. This was a remnant of human sacrifice, the yearly ritual slaughter of the divine king, representative of the summer fertility god. Some say that 7's a lucky number, as he was sacrificed in the seventh month.

Oak has a special place in folklore, being regarded with both affection and awe. The tree was considered a protector, a sanctuary during thunderstorms. It was often planted as the 'village' tree, the centrepoint of a country community. Usually placed by the village green, it provided a meeting place for old cronies and young lovers. Acorns were carried as lucky talismans and blindpulls carved of oak were thought to give the best and longest service. Like all trees, oaks have souls. The Greeks named them hamadryads, picturing them as beautiful maidens. In some English counties they were envisaged as 'oak-men,' but everywhere it was held that, 'Faery folks are in old oaks.'

The vengefulness of ill-treated oaks was legendary. If an oak was cut, it would scream, and the axeman who heard it would die within a year and a day. True to the old faery faith, the spirits of oaks were more active after dusk. Oak coppices particularly, were shunned after sunset. These are managed woods, where the oaks are regularly cut down to ground level. This forces them to produce a crop of new stems after each cutting.

A wronged oak harboured a grudge, "Oak, he do hate!" Anyone who enters an oak wood should be reassured if the leaves give a friendly rustle, but if silence rules the forest, it's a bad omen. The trees might drop a branch on you, or a rain of acorns. If they really take a dislike to anyone, they might follow behind them, stopping still every time their victim looks round, or even close in menacingly from all sides. The only hope of protection, is to wear a criss-cross of iron nails in the sole of each boot.

The wren (*Troglodytes troglodytes*), also called Jenny Wren, the wrannock or stag, shares the seventh month with the oak. This tiny bird is Britain's commonest avian resident, most often seen flitting inside a hedge or flying off, shouting it's 'tic-tic-tic' warning song. The wren, known as the 'King of the Birds,' has been sacred for millennia, and is associated with both Druids and witches. To kill one was extremely unlucky.

The wren was also an embodiment of the sacred king, but while the oak-king was the summer god, the wren was his wintry twin, mythically slain at the winter solstice, to allow the summer to be reborn. In the British Isles and France, the taboo on killing the wren was lifted on Boxing Day, when the folk-custom known as the wren hunt took place. Ritually dressed hunters killed a wren, and carried it, sometimes on a pole, sometimes in a special 'wren-house,' in procession demanding tribute from everyone they met. In some places the bird was taken alive and later released.

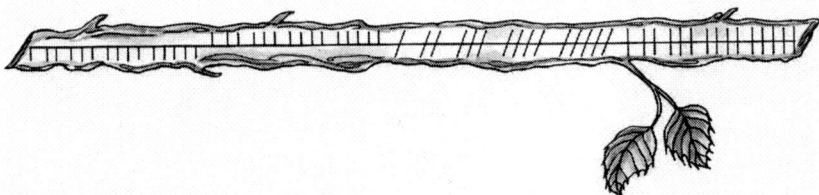

Chapter 10

Holly

Ogham letter: T

Holly (*Ilex aquifolium*), in Celtic tinne, takes eighth place in the ogham cycle. In the ogham calendar it governs July 8th - August 4th, and under the older purely lunar calendar, the eighth Moon month, starting at the eighth New Moon after the winter solstice.

To meet with the spirit of the holly, walk out into a wilderness landscape buried by snow. It crunches underfoot, powder dry, as you march across frozen fields, leaving the shelter of the wind whipped white topped hedgerows. On a mound, near the middle of a field, stands a large holly tree, surrounded by a few low shrubs. As you near it you realise it stands 60 feet high. Its glossy green leaves bear a burden of snow, but you can see their curling sharp points sticking through, dark against the white. You're cheered to see clusters of rich shiny red berries. They resemble drops of blood spattered across the snow. The holly tree exudes a silence. You know it is aware of your presence, unconcerned, yet preferring to be left to its meditations. You see dark specks moving across the snow, a squadron of starlings whirling through the fierce wind, rising and falling, their tiny wings flapping fast. Their leader disappears into the holly branches and perches. Then the others arrive, noisily squabbling and jostling for position as they take their places, safe within the tree's embrace.

When a holly wand is chosen during divination, it signs that you'll find like minds, and get support for whatever projects or ideas you're working on. It predicts that you'll enter into a team spirit, and feel encouraged by sharing mutual goals.

If you're doing something alone, whether a business or sport, holly advises working with others to better your prospects. It omens a good time to deepen understandings in any relationship, but especially favours same sex bonding, friendships rather than love affairs. Sometimes it'll bring an important new companion into your life.

There'll be news of a celebration or an invitation to a gathering, and a general upturn in social activity, with the emphasis firmly on togetherness, good company and fun. Holly favours ventures linked to leisure, entertainment, public houses, brewing, anything that collects people together.

The holly tree, holy tree, holme or hulver bush, is, along with the yew, Britain's most widely known evergreen. It too can form a worthwhile hedge. The tree is slow growing, with extremely dense wood, ideal for stickmaking, carving and inlay work. A holly club makes a fearsome weapon. Birds enjoy the berries but they're dangerous to humans.

Holly was a sacred tree to the ancient Britons, and along with the oak and ash, was one of three trees most commonly planted in druidic groves. These religious associations have lasted into the Christian era. Holly is still a flag of Christmas, the symbolic anniversary of Christ's birth.

It's possible that the name 'holly,' comes from 'holy.' The holly's birth associations are connected to its evergreen nature, which suggests continuing life, and it's berries, still present at the winter solstice, are a reminder of summer's imminent reincarnation and fruitfulness.

The oak, ruler of the previous ogham month, makes a pair with the holly. In societies where the oak god was chief deity, he ruled from the winter to summer solstice, when his dark twin the holly god became ascendant, until he too was eclipsed at the next winter solstice.

In folklore the holly had a masculine character, often twinned with the feminine ivy - the holly boy and ivy girl. The tree was used as a symbol of jollity and good fellowship. In older times, before the pub sign had come of age in all its painted glory, a holly bush was hung outside a building to mark it as a public house. The old public houses were often just that, a normal house that was open to the public, supplying liquor and food. Holly was such a recognised sign of manly fun, that anyone wishing to gather a few friends together for a drink, some stories and songs, would hang a holly bush outside his own house. This association of the holly with merriment could date back to the Saturnalia, the old Roman winter solstice feast, celebrated December 17th-23rd, which included present giving, drunkenness and a general licence for tomfoolery and misrule - nothing changes!

The sinister side of this feast, was that originally, someone was chosen to take the place of the winter holly god Saturn, whose rule was being celebrated. After a jolly fine time, this substitute was ritually sacrificed.

A savage old remedy for chilblains was to thrash the offending limbs with a branch of holly, until blood was drawn.

A bumper crop of holly berries, foretells a hard winter. To chop down a holly tree or burn green holly wood, brings death. Hedgers would often cut back other hedgerow trees and leave the holly growing. It was considered unlucky to bring holly Christmas decorations into the house before Christmas Eve. They had to be brought in by a man, and if they were left up after January 6th, the Devil himself would take up residence. It was unlucky to burn them afterwards.

The bird that shares the eighth ogham month with the holly, is the starling (*Sturnus vulgaris*), otherwise known as the shepster, snow bird, or Jacob. Slightly bigger than a robin, they're one of our most beautiful native birds. The plumage is black, but shines with a metallic green and purple sheen when caught by sunlight. Each feather on the body's tipped with white, and those on the back and head with gold, giving the effect of stars against the night sky.

Starlings are social birds, nesting, feeding and playing together. In folklore they're credited with a martial character. Their flocks are organised like an army with a leader and scouts. In flight they manoeuvre as one, wheeling and dipping in perfect unity like a well trained squadron. They echo both the holly's strength and its link with teamwork and bringing people together.

The white tips on their chest feathers resemble chain mail, and close observation shows that the starlings are spartan little warriors, who pay strict attention to personal cleanliness, indulging in lavish grooming and more than daily bathing.

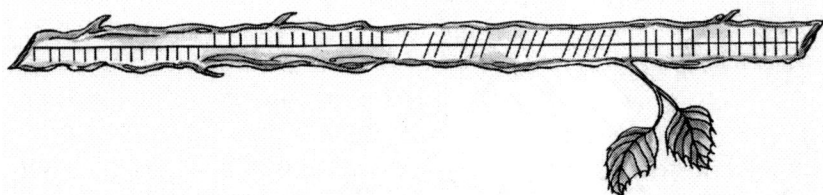

Chapter 11

Hazel

Ogham letter: C

The common hazel (*Corylus avellana*), or in Celtic, *coll*, has ninth place in the ogham cycle. In the ogham calendar it governs August 5th - September 1st, but in the ancient lunar calendar, the ninth Moon month after the winter solstice.

You are entering an ancient forest, part of the landscape of trees that once completely covered Britain. Towering oaks, shady yews and powerful ash trees, make a dense ceiling of living foliage, and underfoot, last year's fallen leaves still feel pleasingly crisp. Deeper in you see hazel trees, their huge serrated leaves making cool shade. You examine the slender branches, and see the promising beginnings of nuts yet to come, small and green, growing in their thousands. The trees are feminine, protecting, crying out for you to dally a while. There's a feeling that they have secrets, or that you'll learn something if you linger long enough. It is a temptation. You gaze up through the sea of branches, and are startled to see an enormous bird, flying high with leisurely beats of its huge wings, head tucked close to its well fed body. This venerable bird is grandfather heron, returning to his roost after a day's fishing by the coast.

If you choose a hazel wand during divination, it heralds news of a birth, sometimes a pregnancy intimately connected to you. If you're trying to start a family, it's the news you're waiting for. A birth or pregnancy will come within a year and a day. If it's not the right time for a child in your life, check your birth control methods. It would be unwise to take chances.

If you're too young, old or just not interested in babies, hazel is generally lucky, signing increase and positive trends. It's also a birth omen of a different kind, bringing a promising beginning, an idea, an innovation in any field, a new course of education, or the chance to give knowledge to others, through writing, the media, or by teaching.

All creative projects will be gifted with the correct spirit for success. Symbolically the nut is the core essence of all art, whether music, literature, theatre or film. It's the seed of inspiration from the Otherworld, from the muse, who ensouls any truly great art.

The hazel tree is an ally, providing useful wood and delicious nuts. The catkins, the tree's flowers, are familiar to every child. Hazels were grown and coppiced for their timber, which was used whenever flexible strong rods were needed, for basket weaving, house building in wattle and daub style, coracle and sheep hurdle making, and for hedging. Hazel rods were woven in among thorn trees to create a dense barrier, although a row of hazels grown as a hedge does the job just as well.

Two crossed hazel twigs are the tools of the dowser. In former times, dowsing was considered a gift, which only special people could practise successfully. The dowser was called in to discover underground water sources, buried treasure or lost property. It's still practised today, and whatever doubters say - it works!

Naturally, such a widespread and familiar tree attracted plenty of folklore. Hazel was lucky to have round the farmyard, as munching on hazel twigs helped fatten the beasts. Also, a whip-stock or drover's gad, a switch used to control animals, made from hazel, protected the herds against malicious spells.

In country districts 'nutting' - collecting the harvest of hazel nuts - was quite an event, often frowned upon by more puritanical minds, due to what was alleged to take place beneath the nut trees. It was an excuse for children and young lads and lasses to disappear into woods, away from parental control, at a time when it was still warm and pleasant enough to get into mischief. Like all harvests in the old countryside, it was a joyous occasion, and if a little love-making went on too, that was quite natural.

Young girls prone to nutting could get a bad reputation. If a maiden went nutting on a Sunday, she was sure to meet the Devil, and the child would come before the wedding! So great were the fertility powers of the hazel, that to eat a nut and wish for a child was often enough to stimulate conception. If a neighbour or relative seems infertile, it's a good idea to give them a present of a large bag of nuts, then a baby's sure to come.

An abundant nut harvest predicts plenty of births within wedlock, or put another way, 'Plenty of catkins, plenty of prams!'

Hazel nuts are associated with Michaelmas Day, September 29th, when they're ready for cracking and eating round the Michaelmas bonfire. The earlier Feast of St. Matthew, was sometimes known as the 'Devil's Nutting Day,' since gathering nuts on this holy day could also provoke a visit from 'Old Nick.'

The heron (*Ardea cinerea*) shares the reign of the ninth ogham month. Otherwise known as the hanser, Jack Hern or Kate Hern, this distinguished looking bird, which seems to be left from the age of the dinosaurs, was sacred to the ancient Britons. The Irish source for bird-ogham the *Book of Ballymote*, gives the crane as the bird of the ninth month. However, although the crane sometimes visits from the continent, it's not a true native species.

The heron is a tall stately bird who ardently stalks ponds and water on its towering legs. They're notoriously proficient fishers, capable of clearing the average garden pond of inhabitants in one or two visits. They nest in heronries, where many birds build their nests close together.

That the heron habitually stands on one leg while fishing has transferred its imagery to the grail romances, where it's associated with Amfortas, the wounded 'fisher-king,' the lame ruler who awaits healing within the Grail castle. Some sources claim he was lamed by a spear thrust through the groin or thigh.

In Classical myth, the crane and therefore the heron, was sacred to the god Mercury, who was inspired to create the first 13 letters of the alphabet, the consonants, by watching cranes flying in formation. This links the bird to the hazel, tree of wisdom, for writing can contain all knowledge, and the ogham letters can divine what's hidden.

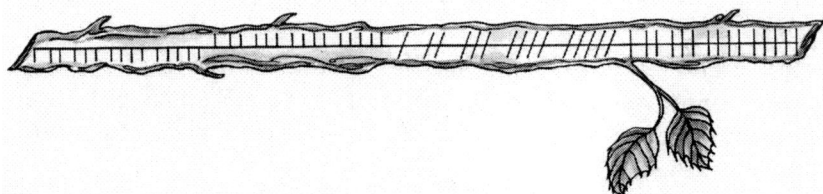

Chapter 12

Crab Apple

Ogham letter: Q/CC

The crab apple (*Malus sylvestris*), in Celtic *quert*, shares ninth place in the ogham cycle, with the hazel. In the ogham calendar it co-rules the ninth ogham month, August 5th - September 1st, or in the older lunar calendar, the ninth Moon month after the winter solstice.

To commune with the crab apple, walk to a Somerset farm in spring. A wooden gate leads through a stone wall into a secluded orchard. Rows of ancient apple trees, three times as high as a man, stretch away towards distant hills. They're in bloom, coloured by clouds of fragrant, pink and white five-star blossom. As you approach the trees, you leave a trail through the thick orchard grass. Their trunks are greyed and fissured, their aged bark's coated with golden lichen, and their branches are bent from seasonal loads of apples. Here and there, as you peer between the gnarled limbs, you glimpse clumps of golden mistletoe. You pause at the far wall, here the farmer has allowed crab apples to grow. They're smaller than the standard trees, slighter but full of character. Their pink blossom is just as beautiful, but you notice they bear thorns, the mark of the wild. As their leaves weave with the wind's breath, you fancy there are voices just beyond your hearing, presences that you can feel but not see, as if another hidden world, lies close to yours. There's a loud clucking near your feet, and as you look down, a scarlet coxcombed rooster strides up complaining of your intrusion. Behind him, his harem of dowdy hens keep on pecking at the grub rich soil.

If you're fortunate enough to select an apple wand during divination, it promises a mystical experience, an insight into the fact that there's more to the universe, than the physical world we perceive with our five earthly senses. This can range from finding an emotional rapport with nature, to sensing what's behind the visual charade of reality. It's been described as the touch of a hand from the Otherworld. It could come as a revelation during meditation, a psychic inspiration, a glimpse of a deceased loved one, even communication with them. It can herald an experience with the faery kingdom, or the forging of a special bond with an animal or bird.

The message is always one of spiritual sustenance, support in adversity, and reassurance. This can come just from gaining an awareness of a spiritual dimension, the sure knowledge that there's something beyond what we know.

The crab apple is native to Britain's hedgerows and forests. It's the ancestor of all cultivated apple varieties. The bitter cider apple from which cider's made, is closest to the wild strain. However, orchardists depend upon the crab apple, as all cultivated apple trees are grown on virile wild rootstocks, with the branches of whichever variety's required, budded or grafted on.

The fruit of the crab apple's valued in its own right, trans- formed into jelly, jam and wine. Fermented crab apple juice, known as verjuice, is an old fashioned remedy for scalds and sprains. The tree's wood is excellent for carving and burns well, providing aromatic smoke.

Old Stone Age hunter-gatherer tribes collected crab apples, and the fruit was probably cultivated before wheat. The apple was venerated by the druids, both as home of the mistletoe, and in its own right. Druidic seers cut their divining rods from its branches, and planted apple groves in which to worship. In Classical civilisation, the apple was sacred to the love-goddess Aphrodite and the sun-hero Hercules. To give an apple was a declaration of love, and their use in spells and divination is recorded through history. As early as 1657, the witches of Somerset were laying curses by giving their victims charmed apples.

The crab apple folklore archive is vast. Its prime association is with the faeries and immortality. Within the apple are seeds of future trees, so the fruit symbolises the goddess' cosmic womb, source of all life.

To see apples on a tree at the same time as blossom was an omen of a death. For a good crop of apples the sun must shine through the apple tree branches on Christmas Day.

At Hallowe'en, apples were used in traditional games, such as 'dukin' for apples, and for the divination of such serious matters as the professions of future husbands. One divination was to peel an apple and throw the skin over the left shoulder. If it remains intact, marriage is a certainty, if it breaks, celibacy is the only outlook.

The trees themselves had spirits, particularly the oldest tree in the orchard, who's known as the Apple Tree Man, or Colt Pixy. Any place where apple trees cluster is a haunt of faeries, and often a gateway to Faeryland, that Otherworld, where faery tribes mingle with the spirits of the dead, awaiting reincarnation. This place is also called Avalon, 'apple-isle,' a mystic island of perpetual twilight, radiant with apple blossoms and heavy laden orchards, the British equivalent of Elysium, the Greek Otherworld, populated by the souls of heroes, sages and kings. It was here that Morgan La Fey transported King Arthur.

The sacred king of some ancient British tribes was presented with an apple by his consort, representative of the Moon goddess, to signal that it was time for his reign to end, and for him to take his place as sacrificial victim.

The chicken, or more precisely, the hen, is given by the *Book of Ballymote* as the bird that shares its ogham letter with the crab apple. This bird has a fond place in our hearts, and increasingly provides more of the protein in the average diet than any red meat.

Once common residents of back gardens as well as farm yards, chickens have been with us since at least Roman times. They were first domesticated in Indonesia, India or Malaysia, and are descendants of the red jungle fowl (Gallus gallus) or its grey relative. Julius Caesar recorded that fowls were never eaten by the ancient Britons, but that they did keep them for entertainment. Whether this 'entertainment' was cock-fighting, remains in doubt. The animals were sacred, and were probably both sacrificial offerings and a means of divination. Predictions would be made from the way specially kept hens ate scattered grain. This was done at Rome too.

Chickens are associated with the harvest season, because of the old custom of letting the hens wander across the newly reaped fields, to peck at the corn left by the harvesters.

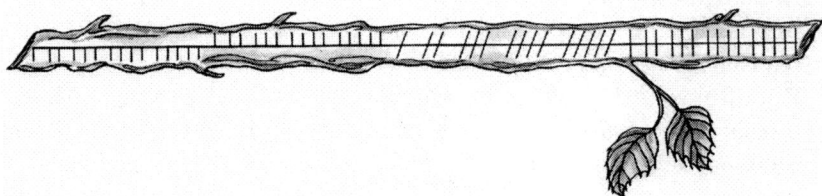

Chapter 13

Blackberry

Ogham letter: M

The blackberry (*Rubus fruticosa*), in Celtic *Muin*, takes tenth place in the ogham cycle. In the ogham calendar it rules September 2nd - September 29th, or in the ancient lunar calendar, the tenth Moon month, starting at the tenth New Moon after the winter solstice.

To feel the touch of the bramble, take a stroll along an old trackway in late September. Choose a dry day so the mud and stone path's not too slippery underfoot, and the dew's dried from the hedgerows that fence it in on each side. The late summer sun's hot, birds and butterflies flutter boldly in its rays. The hedge is not too well cared for. A mass of tangles surround its sturdier inhabitants, elms, hawthorns, black-thorns and hazels. You lean closer, examining the arching, winding, thorned, dangerous stems. There are briars, emblazoned with scarlet rosehips, but even these are overwhelmed by brambles. Old stems an inch thick form a backbone, from which thinner wilder stems grow in all directions. They dangle their lush shiny black fruit enticingly, yet when you reach for one, their thorns bite deep, leaving a red welt. For an instant the brambles seem to be regarding you, a mass consciousness, or coven of individuals working with one purpose. You become sure that if you stayed long enough, their stems would wind round you, pulling you into the hedge. Your attention's drawn by a small yellow bird with a black cap, landing on a swaying bramble stem. It regards you curiously, black eyes gleaming fun, and then springs into the air, uttering its laughing 'teecher, teecher,' cry. You watch it join other great tits, calling as they jump from branch to branch.

Choosing a blackberry wand in divination, means you're in for an interesting time. It brings a phase of joy, unbridled enthusiasm and exhilaration. This can come in the form of intoxication, with drink or narcotics, or with an idea, sex, passion, any impulse that masters the mind and breaks down barriers, quashing what would have previously been personal or cultural taboos.

It can bring a temptation, a chance to practice excess, or a new enthusiasm, for a religion, person or political creed. Something you'll seek to promote and gain converts for.

To get carried away with an impulse brought by the blackberry, could lead to ruin, but channelled wisely, it can transform both yourself and others, opening floodgates to creativity and the dissemination of ideas. Whatever passion it brings, you'll never be the same.

Expect news of a celebration or exciting event, a chance to dance, drink, even love.

The blackberry or bramble grows profusely throughout Britain, rambling through hedgerows and ancient oak forests, and invading gardens persistently. It's remarkably adaptable and mutates readily. Over 2000 varieties have been recognised. All are blackberries, but every one is different.

Blackberry fruits provide a staple of nature's larder. There's nothing quite so delicious as a truly wild blackberry. Brambles are eaten straight from the hedge, baked in pies, or transformed into jellies and wines. Blackberry wine is sweet, red and heady, rivalling the finest Chianti. The fruits develop through three colours, green, red, then purple-black, resembling tiny bunches of grapes.

Muin, the Celtic word, represented here as blackberry, actually means vine. Vine as an ogham tree, is fine in continental Europe, but since it's not native to Britain, blackberry takes its place. The folklore of the two plants is surprisingly similar.

The vine is sacred to the Greek Dionysus, whose worship travelled to Britain with the Romans, who named him Bacchus. The revels of the Bacchantes, his spiritually and alcoholically intoxicated worshippers, were notorious for music, dance and sexual antics. His festivals, under the moon, were a liberation, when all taboos were relaxed. These frolics continued in the witches' Sabbats of mediaeval Europe.

The Ancient Britons had their own wine, beer and cider gods. Some tribes brewed blackberry wine, and celebrated the spirit of the bramble. This bramble-Dionysus was obviously popular, as early Christianity identified him with the Devil, and put prohibitions on the use of blackberries. It was taboo to eat them in many parts of Ireland, right up to the end of the last century.

Theologically, the theory was probably that Satan inspired sin was as prolific and spreading as the bramble, and tasted as sweet as blackberries to the unwary, who would later be torn by its thorny damnations.

The folk-wisdom that it was forbidden to eat blackberries after September 29th, St. Michael's Day, is widespread. After this day they belong to the Devil, and must be left for him as offerings, 'The trail of the serpent is all over them.' Some say the Devil has spat on them. 29th September is the traditional date of Lucifer's fall from heaven.

There is a practical side to this too. Blackberries are best within the ogham blackberry month, September 2nd-29th. After that they spoil. Interestingly, it's the flesh-fly that's responsible for salivating on and spoiling the fruits. The fly's the sacred creature of Beelzebub, Lucifer's second in command.

In Hampshire, fine weather at the end of September and early October, was called a 'blackberry summer.' The blackberry was a faery plant, and whooping cough could be cured by passing the sick child under a bramble arch that's rooted at both ends. It was important to leave an offering of bread and butter. In Ireland, to pass under such an arch and promise to devote oneself to the Devil's service, brought uncanny luck at playing cards. Brambles were often planted on graves to stop the dead from walking, and to keep the sheep off.

The bird that shares the tenth ogham month with the blackberry, is that garden favourite, the great tit (*Parus major*), called fondly by a variety of country names such as bee-biter, tomtit, Joe Bent, black cap, and pick-cheese. This incredibly fast little bird voraciously tucks in at bird tables and feeders, as well as pursuing its natural menu of insects, spiders, buds, seeds and fruit. They have been known to peck holes in milk bottle tops and treat themselves to the cream.

Great tits become more visible in the blackberry month, as the young have fledged and families of birds flock together, constantly on the move for food, raiding the trees for the last of summer's insects.

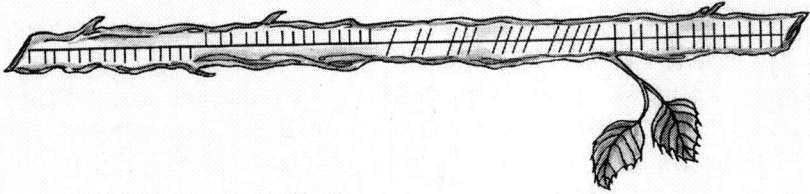

Chapter 14

Ivy

Ogham letter: G

Ivy (*Hedera helix*), or in Celtic *gort*, has eleventh place in the ogham cycle. In the ogham calendar it governs September 30th - October 27th, or if you prefer the older lunar calendar, the eleventh Moon month, starting at the eleventh New Moon after the winter solstice.

To see ivy it at its most impressive, delve into an ancient forest where the oaks grow as wide as a man's arms. Walk there after autumn has culled the leaves from the trees, and only the yews and ivy still glow green. Reaching the old oaks, you see ivy curling up into their branches, winding and clutching, glossy leaves sprouting every way. Up high, bush-like clumps of ivy festoon the branches. To your left there's a vast oak stump, where a venerable forest ancient has fallen. Yet the ivy that clings to it is still vibrant green, bushed out at the stump's top, forming a rounded head, decorated with black berries. Where the ivy emerges from the earth, its crag ridden trunk is over a foot wide. From this, tendrils snake out and up. You wonder if it was the ivy that crushed the life from the centuries old forest king. The more you look around the more you realise that every tree has its ivy burden, clambering upwards, embracing and suffocating. You leave the forest quickly, and retreat to the banks of a sluggish river. At first you think they're white ghosts sliding noiselessly through the water, necks arching with feminine grace. Then a big male swan fixes you with an alert eye, opens his orange beak, and hisses a warning. When you refuse to move, he haughtily ignores you, and has soon swum past.

To draw an ivy wand in divination, promises a challenging time. There'll be restrictions in many life-spheres, obstructions preventing you from doing and achieving your wishes. All progress will be slowed. It may be that your responsibilities restrict you, or outside circumstances, perhaps financial hardship or the actions of others. It could be criticism and antagonism that are stemming your prospects.

If you've enquired of a particular relationship, then that bond will hinder you from doing your will. Whoever you're linking to, whether partner, friend, parent or child, they'll strive to remove your personal freedom, even your liberty to form and express an opinion.

Ivy can point to a case of self-restriction, laziness or lack of inner motivation, holding you back from achieving your true potential. Sometimes the problem is an addiction: drugs, alcohol, gambling, or a destructive relationship.

Whenever ivy binds you, it is vital to change things and break its hold before real damage is done. A tree left in ivy's grip will eventually die.

Ivy needs no introduction. Anyone with a garden or who's

walked the British countryside, will be familiar with this persuasive plant. It is evergreen, loves shade, climbs up anything, clinging on with myriad adhesive rootlets, and can grow up to 100ft long. The flowers are green and emerge in October, the ogham ivy month. The berries, which birds find edible, are black. Ivy leaves grow thickly and are favoured by smaller species that seek sheltered nest sites.

Ivy leaves boiled in lard make an excellent lotion for burns, while a tea made from ivy tendrils complete with leaves, boiled for 3 hours, then left for 24, are said to cure eczema.

The early Christian church forbade the use of ivy as a Christmas decoration. Some people won't have the plant in the house, believing it unlucky. Others will only take it in on Christmas Eve, and insist on it's removal by January 6th. The truth is that ivy was considered to 'bind' evil spirits away, and was sacred to the widely popular god Dionysus, the Roman Bacchus, who's often portrayed wearing a wreath of ivy leaves. Christmas was Dionysus' nativity too, hence the Church's disapproval.

One fabled property of crushed ivy leaves boiled in wine was to relieve drunkenness. Strangely, the mediaeval tipple, ivy-ale, is incredibly intoxicating. Not too long ago, English taverns, had a sign showing an ivy bush painted over their doors. This reassured potential customers of the top qualities of the drink sold within.

In British folklore, ivy was regarded as feminine. The ivy girl of folksong was the counterpart of the holly boy. Symbolically, these figures portray the relationship between the goddess and god of nature, as well as the human battle of the sexes. The female ivy winds round the upright masculine holly, eventually conquering it. It's probable that the ivy was originally sacred to Dionysus' mother, the Great Goddess, and only passed to him by association.

The phallic poles (*thrysus*) carried by the Maenads, Dionysus' heavily intoxicated worshippers, were entwined with ivy, symbolising the vagina's envelopment of the penis. After all Dionysus was a fertility god.

The bird that shares the eleventh ogham month with the ivy, is the mute swan (*Cygnus olor*). This is the swan widely loved, admired and fed by all visitors to British riversides. Unlike its relatives the Whooper and Bewick's swans, it's truly British, and never leaves the country. Up close it is a huge bird 60 inches long. As a teenager I stole a swan's flight feather from a nest occupied by both male and female. When he reared up, flapped his wings and hissed, I ran! They're highly territorial and terrorise other water birds.

The swan is a sacred bird, a transformation of the Moon goddess. You can never be sure if you're dealing with a swan, the goddess, or one of her retinue of immortal handmaidens, or even a faery woman. Some legends tell of swan-maidens, taking off their feather coats and becoming human. If a man could capture the garment, the maiden became his bride until she could secure the return of her 'swan-shift.'

To kill a swan was usually unlucky enough to cause death. However, roast swan was a royal delicacy in the reign of Elizabeth 1st.

A swan was said to sing beautifully just before it released its spirit into the Otherworld. This explains why an artist's last work is called their swan-song.

Zeus made love to Moon goddess Leto in swan form, impregnating her with Apollo and Artemis. The Germanic Valkyries, warrior and Fate goddesses, flew as swans, and the chariot of the Roman love-goddess Venus, was drawn by swans.

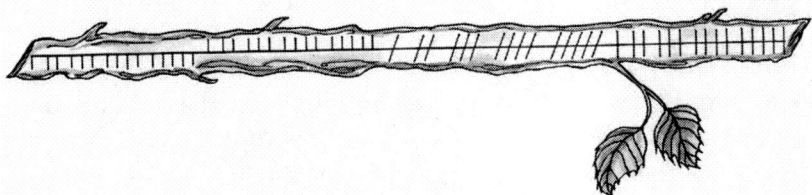

Chapter 15

Wheat

Ogham letter: Ng

Wheat, or some say reed, known as *ngetal* in Celtic, takes twelfth place in the ogham cycle. In the ogham calendar it rules October 28th - November 24th. However, in the older purely lunar calendar, the wheat moon's the twelfth Moon month, only when an intercalary Moon is needed to bind the lunar year back into step with the solar. This occurs every two or three years, and is known as a 'thirteen moon year.' When the year's a 'twelve moon year,' the Wheat Moon's missed out.

To witness wheat in its full glory, choose a high summer day just before harvest. Ramble into arable farmland, where the fields of glowing golden corn stretch far away, rolling with the earth's contours. The wheat stands higher than your knees. Its colour's vibrant and you can smell the rich hay aroma, as it dries in the glaring midday sun. Large wheat ears, plentiful with grain, sway on strong stalks. The next field you enter has already been harvested. It stretches down to a small weaving river, the boundary between water and earth is marked by thick beds of green reeds. You walk over the bare red earth, the hard corn stubble sticking straight up, makes the going tough. Scattered grain, spilled in the cutting and binding, dots the ground. You notice you're not alone. Nearer the water a flock of grey geese are gathering the grain, honking to each other as they move around, graceful with their long necks and stately waddle. They have their young with them, and they follow their parents, copying their actions.

Whenever the wheat straw's selected in ogham divination, it tells that increased responsibility is about to be granted you. This could be within your career environment, religious grouping or community. It emphasises that you're currently receiving, or are about to gain respect, from the people around you.

Wheat's a sign that you've the influence to sway things your way, to make changes in your society. This could be on a local scale or on a national level - that depends on who you are!

It also indicates that your position and power in your current role, have reached their peak. Make the most of this by striving to achieve your goals. Once that peak has passed, as it surely will, you'll not have the same influence, or the opportunities to utilise it.

If you can maintain your authority by wise manoeuvres or playing politics, that's fine, but the consequences of abusing power or holding onto it against the will of the majority, or when you're unable to fulfil the responsibilities it involves, can only lead to a shaming fall from grace.

Wheat is the base ingredient of bread, 'the staff of life.' Most civilisations are based on the growing of wheat or similar cereals, such as oats, barley, rye and millet. All cereals are descendants of wild grasses. The reed too is a grass. The ogham reed is probably (*Phragmites australis*), a tall grass that grows at the edge of rivers, lakes and ponds. Like wheat straw it's used for thatching roofs. Reeds form a dense bed, and can easily block a river if not regularly cleared.

The letter grouping 'ng,' does not occur in any Celtic language. It's use at the beginning of the word 'ngetal' is an artificial rendering of 'getal,' reed, assumed to explain the existence of an ogham letter signifying 'ng.' This is fascinating as it suggests that ogham was learnt from or influenced by a people using another language, perhaps a non-Celtic tribe native to the British Isles. The sound 'ng' is common in languages originating in North Africa.

When I began learning ogham, ngetal fascinated me. It's the only letter that doesn't symbolise a tree. Even the ogham climbers ivy and blackberry/vine can grow to tree size and form dense wooden trunks. The mystery deepened when the old countryman from whom I learnt the system, insisted that 'wheat straw' followed ivy and preceded elder. Interestingly, wheat and reed have mythological similarities.

In Egypt, a North African civilisation which influenced Greece, Rome and Britain, the ruling Pharaoh wielded a reed sceptre as symbol of his power.

Once agriculture had been introduced, Europe's predominant rural pagan cult was the worship of the spirit of the corn, a type of deity sometimes referred to as a 'corn-Dionysus.' His royal sceptre was a wheat straw, as he was manifest in the growing corn. The celebrations of his birth and death formed a festive cycle that survives today. Ploughing, sowing and harvesting all had their festivals. The most famous was the harvest home, celebrated once the corn was safely carted from the field. Thanks were also given to Dionysus' mother, the corn goddess Ceres, an incarnation of the triple moon goddess.

Her ceremonial image was the original corn 'idol' or dolly.
In ancient times royal power was brief as the sacred king was ritually sacrificed after a set period. Originally an incarnation of the alder, oak or ash tree god, among corn growing British tribes he metamorphosed into the earthly representative of the corn god, sacrificed to ensure a rich harvest at Lughnasad, August 2nd.

Reed's the perfect plant to symbolise fleeting royal power in a nomadic pastoral or hunter gatherer fisher society, while wheat's better for a sedentary agricultural people. Perhaps reed was the original but was superseded by wheat straw.

The greylag goose (*Anser anser*) or its domesticated relative, the farmyard goose, is the bird that shares wheat's place in the ogham cycle. The greylag's the only goose to breed in Britain and stay resident all year round. They famously mate for life and reaffirm their love-bonds with intricate ritual dances.

Whereas the wheat straw's the emblem of the corn-god, the goose is sacred to his mother, the goddess in her Full Moon maternal aspect. Who did you think Mother-goose was? German witches were reputed to fly on geese to their Sabbats.

The traditional English meal for Michaelmas, September 29th and sometimes Martinmas, November 11th, was roast goose. Connoisseurs consider they're fatter and better by Martinmas, during the goose's ogham month. This feast of St. Martin, replaced the older pagan Celtic Samhain festival, the ancient New Year and beginning of winter, when the spirits were placated and the future divined. In folklore, oracles were taken from the devoured goose's wishbone.

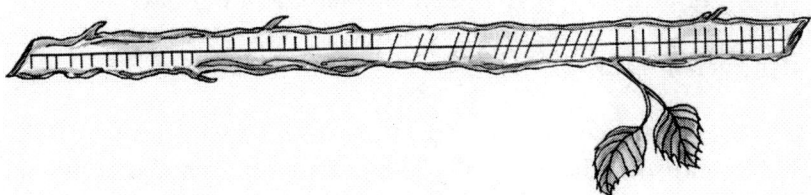

Chapter 16

Elder

Ogham letter: R

The elder (*Sambucus nigra*) or *ruis* in Celtic, has thirteenth place in the ogham cycle. In the ogham calendar it governs November 25th - December 22nd. In the ancient lunar calendar, it's the twelfth Moon month, beginning at the twelfth New Moon after the winter solstice. If, as happens every two or three years, an intercalary Moon month is inserted after the eleventh Moon, the Elder Moon becomes the thirteenth Moon month.

To seek out the elder, wander away from the houses of men and down to a freshwater lake, when the cold water ripples with an October breeze. Just away from the water's edge where the trees begin to get thick, there's an old elder, her many trunks towering to above head height. Each sprouts many long branches, all bent under the weight of numerous shiny black berries, clustered in groups like bunches of miniature grapes. They taste fruity but dry and stain your fingers and mouth a rich purple. The tree's old bark is lined and wrinkled like a grandmother, and you feel the presence of her ancient soul.

There's another sensation too, that she is aware of you. Her leaves dance with the wind and her river soil scent surrounds you. You instinctively know that she can be a very strict grandmother. Above you hear the unmist-akable cawing of rooks. They're flying high back to their roost, lazily gliding, wings stretched out, their tips resembling long black fingers. They call to a straggler, who flaps hard to catch up, calling for the others to wait.

If you pluck an elder wand during divination, it predicts that there's something of importance soon to be revealed to you. This will be knowledge that'll come through experience or the words of others. It'll be of benefit if you act wisely, and respect the pathway the gods are opening for you, even if it's a difficult one. As with any divination, the idea is to be warned. Once the elder has alerted you to potential changes, preserve your strength and cease any activity or plan which may prejudice your well- being.

When the elder appears you'll gain insight into your own situation, that of someone close, or even the workings of the world. It signs an increase in wisdom, which can be defined as knowledge refined through experience and contemplation, not the mere possession of facts or opinions. So, as wisdom's an insight into truth, it's also a glimpse of the divine, which is absolute truth,

The elder, ellhorn, ellan, fire or pipe-tree, has long been used by man. Almost every part of it has medicinal value: bark, buds, flowers, berries, and leaves. Elder is 'the medicine chest of the country people.' Elderflower tea destroys coughs. Elderberries make a brooding red wine, and the white flowers, a musky white. The tree's valuable in hedges and its hollowed stems make excellent blow-pipes. In ancient times, wind instruments were carved from them. The flowers have a narcotic smell, while the berries are rich in iron.

The elder's a tree of witchcraft and magic, revered in folklore as home to the Elder tree-mother, and as a sanctuary for faeries and witches. The Elder tree-mother's an incarnation of the old Queen of Faery, the dark goddess or crone aspect of the triple Moon goddess, a deity feared as mistress of sorcery and prophecy. As tree of the thirteenth ogham month, the elder's the goddess in her role as layer-out of the deceased. In this month the year ends at the winter solstice, after which time the god of the waning year was ritually sacrificed.

No wise woodsman would cut an elder without removing his hat, kneeling, and saying, "Lady Elder, grant me some of your wood, and when I'm dead, I'll give you some of mine." Many people refused to burn elder wood, believing it terrifyingly unlucky.

A child put into an elder cradle became the property of the faeries, who'd pinch it black and blue, or of their dark Queen, the Elder tree-mother. She'd pull the youngster out of its bed and claim it as her own. She even haunted households who dared to fashion furniture from her wood. Strangely, many British cottagers planted elders by their homes to protect against faeries and witches, as if by giving these elder spirits a dwelling, they protected their own. Elder leaves put up over entrance doors and windows, on April's last day also give mystical protection.

The rook (*Corvus frugilegus*), nicknamed the bare-faced or white-faced crow, church parson, or in Cornwall, Bran, shares the thirteenth ogham month with the elder. It's a bird that to many people is symbolic of the British countryside. As the old rhyme says, "Oh! The merriest bird the woods ever saw. Is the rook with the wild caw, caw."

The rook is a member of the crow family, distinguished from the carrion crow only by gregarious life-style, a bare patch of grey skin behind the beak, and baggier thigh feathers. The birds feed, roost and nest in flocks. Their bickering, laughter and windy day acrobatics make them a joy to watch.

Folklore tells of the rooks' parliament, when the flock meets to make decisions, arrange pecking order and punish miscreants. Rook habit of choosing tall trees near good pastureland to build in, means they often nest near human dwellings. It was customary when taking over a house, to inform the local rooks and reassure them that you wanted them to stay, and would keep them safe from strangers. They also had to be told of a death in the family. If not, they could get restless and leave their rookery, and no house deserted by its rooks can ever prosper. They guard the house and warn of approach. It's said that no rook will work at its nest on Ascension Day.

Some farmers cull their rooks to keep numbers down - a particularly useless strategy which causes the birds to breed more freely and recruit new flock-members from elsewhere. They do eat grain, seed and fruit, but how many crops would be lost entirely if the rooks didn't gorge on wireworms and leatherjackets?

The rooks share the elder month, as in December they're more visible, feeding well, playing in the blustering winds and inspecting their nests ready for the next year. They announce to the other birds when it's time to nest. Juvenile rooks just out of the nest, but before they take their first tumbling flight, wait on the tips of nearby branches to be fed and are known as 'branchlings.'

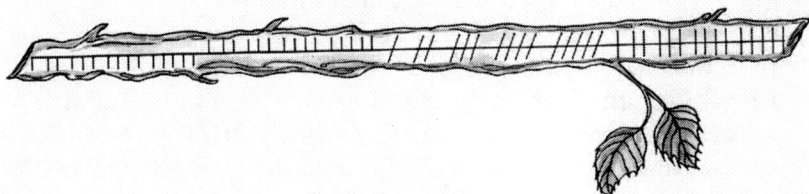

Chapter 17

Scots Pine

Ogham letter: A

The scots pine (*Pinus sylvestris*), or *ailm* in Celtic is the sixteenth ogham tree. Ailm's more properly the old word for silver fir (*Abies alba*). However, that tree's not native to the British Isles, and oral tradition replaces it with the indigenous scots pine. The previous fifteen ogham trees ruled solar months or Moon months and all represented consonants in the ogham alphabet. The scots pine begins the cycle of five vowels, and governs only one day in every year, the winter solstice, which is usually December 22nd. The ancient Britons considered that each day began at sunset. So this ogham rules from sunset on the longest night, until last light on the day after.

To locate a group of scots pines, walk an old straight track in the north of England in mid-winter. You can see them straightaway. Far off, three trees rise together from a time worn tumulus. As you get nearer, you can appreciate their height. You climb the mound and they tower erect over you, supported by massive trunks. Looking upwards, you see their green needle leaves swaying in the chill wind. The sky above is icy blue, and you feel that the trees emanate a similar austerity, a sense of removal from the pettiness of the life swirling about their feet. You gaze away over the fields. On the bare brown, recently ploughed earth you see shapes moving - birds feeding. As they wander nearer, you see they're lapwings, busily probing the soil, their dark green feathers reflecting the distant winter sun.

If you draw a scots pine ogham wand, it reveals that you need to be true to yourself, your goals and sensibilities. It's a sign of purity and individuality, so if you base decisions on higher perspectives, your path will be correct. It would be unwise to rely on anyone, or any advice.

It's a mystical symbol, predicting the emergence of a new spiritual path, or a marker point on one that already exists. The spiritual impulse of the scots pine is towards transcendence and altruism, purification and concentration on the divine.

It can foretell a time alone, or a period where you would grow more as a person if you focused on where you were going, rather than the joys and pitfalls of relationships. The tree grants a healing space, sometimes a retreat from the world, a symbolic return to innocence.

The silver fir is a tree of the central European highlands, prominent in places such as the Black Forest in Germany. It's the original Christmas tree, and therefore links well with the winter solstice. It's the tree of Wotan, the Germanic Odin. Being evergreen it symbolises that life's latent in nature, even in the frozen winter. The winter solstice is celebrated as the turning point of the year, after which the days begin to grow longer, and summer becomes imminent.

Ironically, the silver fir became quite common in Britain, due to the craze for planting exotic trees in the 19th century. It even grows in the wild. The tree's primary mythic association is with birth. This is fitting as the winter solstice marked the sun's rebirth and the nativity of the divine child, whether called Dionysus, Mithras, Attis, Jesus or Horus. In the Dionysian processions, phallic batons were carried, tipped with pine cones. They also played a role in the mysteries of Mithras. In Greece the tree was sacred to Artemis, patroness of childbirth. The Trojan horse was said to be fashioned of silver fir, the favoured wood of the Trojan Moon goddess, Athene.

The scots pine shares much of the silver fir's mythology. It is Britain's only large native conifer, a remnant of the Caledonian pine forests that covered much of Scotland in prehistoric times. Scots pines can reach 120ft in height. Forests of these majestic trees form a unique habitat, sheltering pine marten, wildcat, capercaillie and crested tits, wildlife that's scarce in other environments. The tree's wood is marvellous for furniture, fencing, building and making charcoal. It's also a prime source of turpentine, resin and tar. The torches that lit stone age temples, mediaeval banqueting halls and stately homes throughout the Highlands, were scots pine.

In folklore the scots pine is a lucky and friendly tree, offering sanctuary to travellers and marking sacred sights of significance, usually burial mounds. Pines were planted as part of the system of leylines that criss-crosses Britain. These ancient tracks followed the invisible veins of earth energy, providing easy navigation for prehistoric travellers. Because of their height, scots pines were planted at relevant points as visual guides. As long as you were walking towards a pine, you were on the ley and on course.

Before the coming of the trains, livestock was moved from Scotland, Wales and other areas, to market in London or the midlands, on foot. In charge of the travelling herds were men called drovers. Many of their 'drove-roads' were leys, and pines continued to be grown as way-markers. Farmhouses would plant a clump of pines, both for the luck and to alert visiting drovers to the fact that they had grazing available for their beasts.

The bird that shares the winter solstice with the scots pine is the lapwing (Vanellus vanellus), otherwise known as the peewit or green plover, a striking bird, white underneath and iridescent green on its back. They were once common on cultivated land, but due to their custom of nesting on the ground, modern farming methods have driven them to wilder places to raise their young.

In winter, lapwings flock together and can be seen feeding in the fields. In folklore the bird plays the role of guardian of the mysteries. Adult birds feign injury to lead predators away from their nests. Symbolically the egg contains the secret of creation, and its great potential.

Others say the correct bird is that beautiful but grim reaper the magpie (*Pica pica*), marked black for the long nights and white for the embracing snow, a fitting bird for the time of mid-winter sacrifice. Although they're omnivorous, it's the magpie's role in nature to harvest sickly young birds and ill defended nests. The magpie's a member of the crow family and is as mischievous and intelligent as its cousins. The magpie's white and black, but in the right light, their black feathers sparkle metallic green.

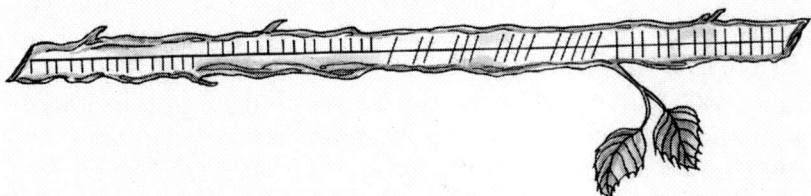

Chapter 18

Gorse

Ogham letter: O

Gorse (*Ulex europaeus*), or *onn* in Celtic is the seventeenth ogham tree, and second in the sequence of vowels. It governs the second marker point of the solar calendar, the spring equinox, usually March 21st. At this equinox, the day and night are equal in length. Beyond it, the light has won the battle over darkness, and the days become increasingly longer than the nights.

To find gorse, choose a high summer day, when the air is laden with scent, and the insect hum is constant as they buzz between flowers. Climb above the verdant shady forest, onto the sparse heath where the trees grow smaller, stunted by howling winds, and purple heather competes with rocks for root-space. In groups or solitary, gorse bushes jut from the earth, marked by their glorious display of flaming yellow blooms. They're as high as your head, some stretching taller than others, as if reaching for the sky. You see that every leaf's a sabre sharp thorn, with the flowers tucked protectively among them. You feel their beauty, but sense that to touch, even in gentle exploration, would be painful. The trees are silently observing you, reading you. Far off in the crystal sky a large black bird circles above a faraway lake, and then slowly descends onto its mirror-like surface. You know from it's size that it's a cormorant and not a crow.

Pick a gorse wand during an ogham divination and you're in for an interesting time. It omens a flirtation, new relationship or affair, based on sexual attraction rather then emotion. Your passions will be raging, and if left unchecked, they'll lead you into a dangerous liaison.

If you involve with a lover, it may be fun but it won't last. Whoever you link to would be fickle, unreliable and could tempt you from your path. If you follow the libertine urges of gorse, your values risk corruption.

It warns that your status or reputation is challenged, or about to become so. Your behaviour, untidiness, promiscuity, or just lack of self-control is endangering the respect others have for you.

Gorse, otherwise known as whin, furze, broom or frey, is unmistakable, burning with yellow flowers and armed with countless lacerating spines. It can grow on difficult soils, tolerating sand, acid, high winds and sea air, but is best known for thriving on heaths.

Dried gorse wood makes excellent kindling, producing extreme heat very quickly. In hot summers this tendency's responsible for devastating heath fires. In some areas gorse was cultivated and harvested every three years for use as fuel. Once burnt the ashes were utilised as a top quality alkaline manure.

Cattle are partial to the young shoots. It makes a good hedge but is susceptible to frost. Many smaller birds, including linnets, stonechats, whinchats and Dartford warblers, nest in gorse for protection.

Golden gorse blooms have a heady scent that attracts bees. It flowers heavily in March and April, and can stay in bloom throughout the year. These flowering and protective qualities are alluded to in the saying, 'While the gorse is in flower, Britain will never be conquered.'

Gorse produces blackish pods full of seeds. On hot summer days these dry out and burst with a cracking noise, scattering their cargo.

In folklore, gorse is linked to the faeries, marking their dancing places. There's always a confusion or identification in folk-memory between the faeries, witches, and followers of the old pagan religion. Faeries are the gods, elementals and spirits worshipped or invoked in the ancient rites, and the witches are sometimes pagan priests or their congregation, othertimes memories of spell casting goddesses. After the political ascendance of Christianity, the meetings of older cults had to be held far from the homes of men, for fear of persecution. Gorse grows in wild places, deserted heaths, ideal for the revels of the old religion.

The faeries' dances/witches' sabbats were often Dionysian, taking place at night and featuring intoxication and sexual licence. Still pagan, but perhaps innocently so, the folk festivals frowned on by 17th century Puritans, involved youngsters of both sexes heading away from their homes and authoritarian control, out into wilder gorsier places. Whether this was 'bringing in the May,' or 'nutting' in September, human nature always tends towards doing what comes naturally.

The spirit of the tree, the gorse-faery was reputed to be a charming but untidy and irresponsible female. This is easy to understand when the unkempt appearance of the bushes is considered. Their thorns do collect debris, such as leaves in autumn.

A bough of blooming gorse was presented to any woman who's behaviour was putting her reputation in jeopardy. Another old custom was to include a spray of gorse in the bridal bouquet, to increase sexual appetite.

The wisesaw, 'Kissing's out of fashion when the whin's out of blowth,' humorously refers to the fact that gorse's always in bloom.

The bird that shares the spring equinox with gorse, is the cormorant (*Phalacrocorax carbo*), otherwise known as the sea crow or gormer. It's easy to see why this bird was called the 'sea crow.' Although they have white patches on thighs and throat, their other feathers are black, so in flight they do resemble huge crows.

Cormorants inhabit sea shores, nesting on cliffs, islands and tall trees. They're excellent fishers, diving below the water to snatch their prey. They also fly inland to raid rivers, lakes and lochs, and can often be seen perched on a rock holding out their wings to dry. Mysteriously their feathers, unlike those of gulls and ducks, are not waterproof and need thorough drying.

Mythologically the cormorant, along with the gull, raven and hooded crow, was one of the forms taken by the Celtic dark goddess, the crone of the waning Moon, the ferocious Fate, war and witch mother. In Scotland she was known as the Cailleach, and March 25th, now Lady Day, was formerly Cailleach Day, her sacred festival. Until 1599 it was also New Year's Day. This came from the choice of March 25th as a convenient date on which to celebrate the spring equinox, the beginning of summer's victory over winter, day over night. The Dark goddess of winter was feted as her power began to wane.

In some seafaring communities the cormorant was a bird of ill-omen foretelling a wreck or death at sea. Milton went so far as to see it as a likeness of the Devil.

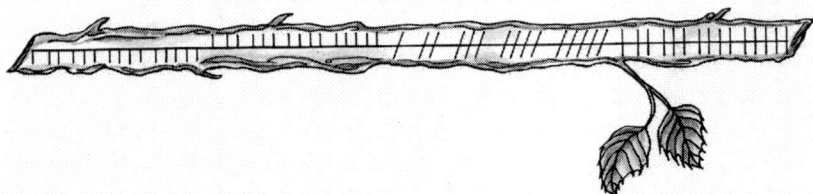

Chapter 19

Heather

Ogham letter: U

Heather (*Calluna vulgaris*), or *ur* in the old Celtic tongue, is the eighteenth ogham tree, and has third place in the sequence of vowels. It governs the third marker point of the solar year, the summer solstice, normally June 21st. This is midsummer, time of the longest day and shortest night. After this, the sun begins to decline again, the days grow shorter and the nights longer.

To be enchanted by heather, head for West Somerset hills in summer. Where they rise from the green fields, pastureland fades into the purple fire of their gently climbing heights. You know before you reach it, that the heather's alive with bees, droning their songs of pollen and honeycomb. Gorse towers here and there, in clumps like spine turreted castles. You find an old track and follow it towards the hill's top. Other tiny paths, trod by countless non-human feet, run winding through the miniature shrub forest. As the sun climbs higher you smell the heather's flowers. High above the world you feel intoxicated by the summer scents and intense heat. You sense that the heather's consciousness surrounds you, that the countless plants are one, and you're among them, known by them, welcome yet watched. There's a sense of far awayness, of a place truly wild, unpolluted by too much of man's tread. An otherness underlies it all - anything could happen. You could become lost and wander feral and possessed forever in this faery place, never returning to the security of human habitations. A movement draws your eye. A small dark bird climbs into the sky from somewhere among the heather. It's high noted music begins immediately. Eventually it hovers, a dot in the sky, performing its aria to the sun and creation. It sobers you to know that this tiny skylark, would sing whether you were present or not.

To select a heather wand during divination, can be unsettling. It brings cycles of change, breaking up the ground to transform current situations and create new ones. These fresh situations may not be what you envisaged or planned for.

Heather can be a sign of a move, a change of location for you or the company you work for, urged by circumstances. Alternatively, someone else may leave home, perhaps a partner or grown child. A group of friends or work colleagues may disperse and go their separate ways.

Whatever is occurring, you may feel insecure or disorientated. The only way through is to adapt to the changes, go with the flow and make the most of the opportunities, that are bound to arise as a result of this evolutionary phase.

Heather, sometimes known as ling, is a woody shrub that grows throughout the British Isles, anywhere that the soil's acidic. It's best known for accompanying gorse, colouring barren hills and heaths with carpets of purple blooms. These flowers attract bees and give a distinctive flavour to their honey. Birds feast on heather seeds and red grouse browse on the young shoots. White heather's rarer, but occurs naturally and is the same species as the purple.

In former times, heather was an important source of fuel, its wood burning fiercely and easily. The stems were woven into baskets, and were sometimes used as bedding or material for thatching. Heather stems are still collected, dried and bound together to make the 'brush' part of traditional brooms. Heather brooms are for sweeping indoors. Yard brooms have brushes of birch. The legendary heather ale is a delicious and intoxicating drink.

Heather has given its name to heaths, technically a large open area populated by shrubby plants, usually including plentiful heather. The term 'heathen,' meaning a worshipper of the old gods, was born from the fact that people living in isolated communities, on heaths etc, far from 'civilisation,' were among the last to be converted to Christianity. They were considered to be wilder and harder to convince.

Beliefs about the 'wildness' of heath dwellers pre-dates Christianity too. The 'Old People,' aboriginal non-Celtic tribes, were eventually pushed from the more fertile lands, and being pre-agricultural hunter-gatherers or herders anyway, readily took to living in the more deserted landscapes. These peoples were feared as magicians and were sometimes confused with faery beings.

Heather is sacred to the goddess in amorous and destructive mood. In some traditions she chooses her consort at mid-summer, and it's he who beheads his predecessor before replacing him. Her new love's the winter god, while his vanquished foe's the summer deity. The plant is also linked to Isis of Egypt, and Venus Erycina of Rome and Sicily.

In folklore the commoner purple heather is usually considered unlucky, and many people won't have it brought into the house. The feeling is that it brings change, even breaks up a home. The lucky heather sold by knowing Romany gypsies was always white, as this is the colour of purity, and offers protection from such bad luck. Unfortunately I have it on good authority, that because of its rarity, white heather was gathered in a special way. It started life as purple heather, got soaked in horses' urine, and was then dried white in the sun. Watch what you buy!

The skylark (*Alauda arvensis*), otherwise known as the laverock, lintwhite, alovette, or Our Lady's hen, is the bird that shares the summer solstice with the heather. This bird, which is slightly smaller than a starling, has a tiny crest and feathers of three shades of brown. It's beautiful in it's own way, but is famed for it's song and behaviour. A real country bird, found in and around fields, meadows, moors and beaches, the skylark nests and raises its chicks on the ground.

They sing nearly all year, but are more noticed in spring and summer. The bird rises from the ground, ascending almost vertically, wings fluttering, several hundred feet into the air, constantly uttering its warbling distinctive song. It then hovers, still performing, for minutes at a time. Eventually he or she sinks to the ground, singing on the descent too.

Folklore thinks of the skylark as a happy bird. Most commonly seen rising over a ripening field of wheat, they're redolent of increase and prosperity. The bird's soaring vertical ascent and magical song make it sacred to the sun. Like tiny solar priests they clamber towards the burning orb, chanting its praises.

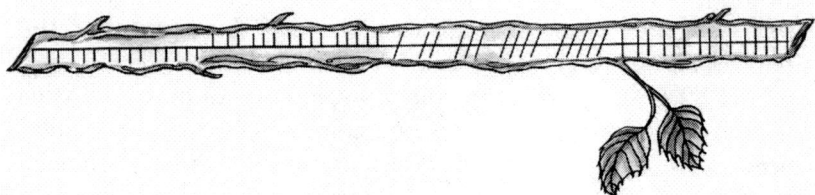

Chapter 20

Aspen

Ogham letter: E

The Aspen (*Populus tremula*), or in Celtic, *eadha*, is the nineteenth ogham tree, and has fourth place in the sequence of vowels. It rules the fourth marker point of the solar calendar, the autumn equinox, usually September 21st. At this time, night and day are exactly equal. Afterwards the hours of darkness stretch longer.

To uncover the aspen's secrets, head for the Scottish highlands, to a forest's edge, where the trees are fewer in number. Many of these trees are aspens. It's a clear bright day in late April, and the wind still bears a distinct chill. As the breathe of the breeze plays across the landscape, the aspens shiver as one, leaves rustling, moving, speaking a wordless language of sound. You strain your ears as if their meaning's not too far distant, just beyond your senses. The leaves on the slender branches, the way they divide the light, invoking shadow dances, their companionable talk, set you thinking of other days, other feelings, perhaps from long ago, you don't quite know when, as if emotions stayed while memories fled. You can't exactly perceive whether the recollection is happy or sad. A distant trumpeting sound, snaps the aspens' spell. Far away, flying low, you can see a flock of large long necked birds. They travel in formation, sometimes calling, sometimes falling silent. It's the last of the whooper swans, migrating to their summer breeding grounds, travelling north towards the Arctic.

To choose an aspen wand in divination, summons an emotional state rather than a specific event. It signs that you'll be feeling the touch of that greater reality, which lies behind life's veil. This could manifest as nostalgia, a bittersweet vibration of sadness and happiness, or an overwhelming awareness of physical mortality and the inevitability of time and Fate. You'll sense the ever changing nature of creation, and the presence of an eternal reality beyond the material world - a poetry of meaning within one sensation, an instinctive, inexpressible knowledge, a communion with the spirit realm. It can be a sign of grief, of mourning, sometimes caused by knowing a life-phase is drawing to a close, or reflecting on the far past and experiencing again its emotions, perhaps in a different way, or with a new deeper awareness.

The aspen is a member of the poplar family, common in northern Britain, but quite often found further south. It's sometimes called the white beam or white poplar, although confusingly, both these names are the correct terms for two completely different species.

The aspen is well known for its trembling leaves. This occurs due to the leaf stalks being flat rather than round and therefore offering more wind resistance. The bark's silvery in colour and furrows with age, forming an attractive black diamond pattern. For this reason aspens are often grown as ornamental garden trees. They have lovely amber leaves in autumn and catkins in spring. The tree is not big enough for the timber to be used commer-cially, and the countryman's taboo that aspen wood should never be used for farming or fishing implements, still stands.

In folklore the aspen is considered unlucky and its trembling is associated with grief and mourning. Several Christian folk-legends have grown up around this. Some say the cross on which Jesus was crucified was of aspen, and that the tree has mourned ever since. Others claim that on the day of the crucifixion, all nature wept and groaned except the aspen, who exclaimed that all the trees and flowers were free from sin. However, shortly afterwards, the tree was seized with trembling and will do so until Judgement Day. Another tale tells how the holy family, Mary, Joseph and Jesus, while fleeing King Herod's baby holocaust, entered a forest. All the trees bowed down to them, except the proud aspen, who was promptly cursed by young Jesus.

More amusingly, it's been suggested that the aspen's leaves are never still or quiet, because they're the transformed tongues of women.

The aspen failed to bow to the holy child because it was sacred long before, to the god Heracles. He claimed the tree as his own after performing his twelfth labour, the capture of the three headed dog Cerberus, guardian of the Underworld's gates.

On his way back through Hades, Heracles wove himself a wreath of aspen leaves, plucked from the tree that grew by the pool of Memory - the waters from which souls initiated into the mysteries drink, to retain awareness of previous incarnations upon rebirth. The heat from Heracles' brow turned the underside of the leaves white.

This aspen grew in Hades as it was originally the sacred tree of the Underworld deity Persephone, goddess of regeneration. In her honour, the leaves are dark on one side, symbolising death, light on the other, indicating life - two sides of one eternal coin. Fate is the wind which blows the leaves from side to side.

The whooper swan (*Cygnus cygnus*) is the bird that shares the autumn equinox with the aspen. This swan's a yearly visitor to Britain, flying here to escape the Arctic winter's harshness. After the autumn equinox the swans prepare for their journey, usually arriving here around October. They leave Britain in April, to raise their cygnets in the arctic summer. Some birds stay, nesting in northern Britain or on isles such as Orkney.

The whooper swan is the second swan of the ogham cycle. Unlike its tamer cousin the mute swan, a familiar sight on urban lakes and rivers, the whooper is a bird of the wilderness, of deserted lochs and snow blasted moors. The name whooper derives from its loud trumpeting call.

Much of the folklore linked to the whooper is identical to that concerning the mute swan. To destroy a swan is extremely unlucky. There's a tradition that some people are reborn as swans, usually virtuous young women. The number of Celtic myths with swan themes, such as, 'The Children of Lir,' and the 'Wooing of Etaine,' and the transformations they record, between faery, human and swan, attest to how revered these birds were.

At the northern end of the whoopers' migrations, they were also held sacred. Siberian tribesmen would pour a drink offering to the first swan to appear in spring, and the women would offer it a prayer. Interestingly, the fact that it's the women who communicate spiritually with the birds, reminds us that all swans are sacred to the Great Goddess.

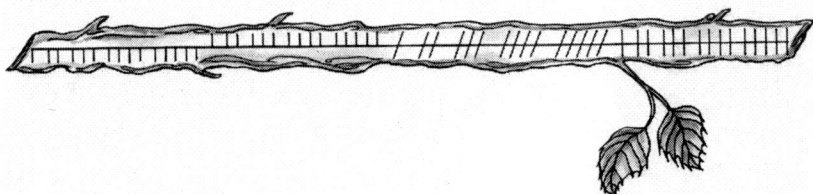

Chapter 21

Yew

Ogham letter: I

The Yew (*Taxus baccata*), or in Celtic, *idho*, is the twentieth ogham tree, taking fifth place in the sequence of vowels. It governs a single day, winter solstice eve, the day before the winter solstice.

To shelter in the reassurance of a yew, choose an early summer's day, and saunter down to a village churchyard, where the old stone church is built on an ancient mound. The churchyard's thick with crumbling graves, bobbing like sails on a sea of undulating grass. Here and there a yew towers, rivalling the church steeple. One ancient specimen stands central, stretching as wide as it is tall. Beneath it's huge limbs the shade is dense. You sit and meditate in it's blanketing peace, feeling safe and drowsy. A slight breeze blows its protecting branches. You sleep and dream of mountains that bask in the sunlight of a Scottish summer. In your dream an eagle flies down to her vast untidy nest, carrying a strip of flesh in her mouth. As she arrives a head bobs up, and her solitary chick, covered by thick white down opens its yellow beak to receive the much needed nourishment. You awake, the chick's shrill cries still echoing through your mind.

To draw a yew wand during ogham divination, is symbolic of a coming loss, and the hope of new beginnings. It can sign a bereavement or the end of a situation, but reminds that imminent in all endings is the knowledge of eternity. If it's a person, or other living thing that takes the journey to the Otherworld, then their soul, the true essence of the individual rather than the physical husk, continues. Should it be your career, or a relationship that undergoes transformation, you'll be able to continue in another work-field, or within a fresh emotional union.

Great change leads our thoughts to explore spiritual dimensions, muse on Fate, our purpose in life and reincarnation. So yew can also signify a growing interest in the mysteries, magic or the occult.

The yew, fifty feet high, with glorious dark, evergreen needles, elegant orange-scarlet bark, and myriad crimson cup berries, is a familiar sight. The tree's extremely long-lived. Some famous specimens have reached an age of two thousand years and are still flourishing healthily.

Yew wood is extremely strong and elastic. The lethal English longbow, which drove arrows through the armour of the French knights at the battle of Agincourt in 1415, was of yew. Before iron became common, yew timber was utilised as probably the next hardest substance.

Birds eat the berries. Their scarlet flesh is safe, but it's the seeds within which are poisonous. Also, both bark and foliage are toxic. Strangely, yew clippings are now in demand for use in the treatment of certain cancers.

Irish yews, whose branches grow upwards, are all descendants of one female yew from Fermanagh, Ireland, grown in 1780. The horticultural term for this shape is fastigate.

Yew hedges are slow growing but form an attractive dense barrier. They're also used in topiary - the art of pruning trees into various shapes, mostly animals or birds.

In folklore the prime association of the yew is with death, and the village graveyard, with its slumbering church guarded by stately yews, is part of what is 'forever England.' The yew was inherited by Christian tradition. They were originally cultivated by the druids, who planted them as sentinels around their temples and burial places. The early church adopted these sacred enclosures and their trees for their own use. Many churchyard yews date from druidic times or are descendants of these trees. A churchyard yew at Coldwaltham, West Sussex, is reported to be 3000 years old, and was probably planted by druid gardeners.

The druids held the yew sacred for many reasons. The long life-span and evergreen habits of the tree, symbolise eternity and the immortality of the soul. Whereas deciduous trees like hawthorn or ash, seem to 'die' in autumn, and are reborn in spring, the yew's greenness is perpetual, echoing the soul's continuation through many summers and winters, and lives and deaths.

To the druids, physical death was only a gateway to rebirth, so the yews growing in places of burial, promise the bereaved that their loved ones will be reborn. In the ogham cycle the tree's day is placed just before the sun is born again at the winter solstice.

However, I have heard one old wag suggest, "They be planted in churchyards because they do thrive on the dead."

It was common for yews to be planted outside farms and homesteads to act as guardian spirits. They also perform this role when planted within graveyards, watching over the sacred ground and the souls passing to the Otherworld.

In Greece and Italy the yew was sacred to Hecate, the old prophetic and sorcerous witch goddess, crone of the waning Moon, eldest of the Fates and mother of all creation. Astrologically thinking herbalists, put the tree under the mantle of Saturn, the god of the old world, and in witch-legend, consort of Hecate, under her title Ops, or Saturna.

The bird that shares winter solstice eve with the yew, is the eaglet, the young of the golden eagle (*Aquila chrysaetos*). This choice of an immature bird to represent this old feast, is especially symbolic.

The importance of the eaglet as opposed to the eagle, is in the behaviour of the young bird. Eagles usually hatch two eggs. The parents devote every care on their hungry offspring, but it's rare that more than one eaglet survives. The strongest of the twins either snatches the lion's share of the food and starves the weaker, or actually pushes it out of the nest. So, although the eaglet emblemises youth and hope, it reminds of life's struggles and the passage to the Otherworld and further rebirth.

Mythically the eagle is a royal bird, totem of the tribal god and his human representative/incarnation, the divine king. In some ancient cults, a sacred king only ruled one half of the year. The winter king was ritually slain and supplanted by his twin, who ruled the summer. Here, the eaglets enact the conflict between the royal twins and the triumph of the stronger.

The eagle as royal bird is a motif that stretched from Babylon to Greece and Rome. Further west in Britain and other Celtic lands, it was more the crow/raven or the wren that were royal birds.

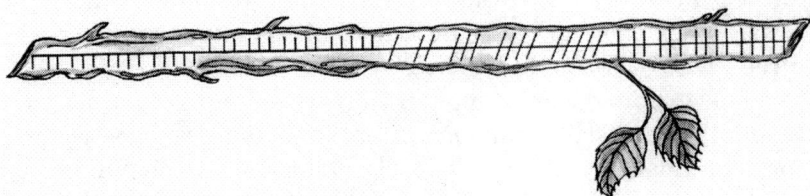

Chapter 22

Mistletoe

Which tree is not a tree? Mistletoe (*Viscum album*) is the 21st and last tree of the ogham cycle. It has no letter or phonetic value, but it is all letters, as it is the breath that forms them. It rules December 23rd, the extra day, the day set apart from the rest of the year due to its sacred and sacrificial nature. The elder governs the 13th ogham month, ending December 22nd, while the birch is the tree of the 1st ogham month, beginning December 24th. So December 23rd belongs to neither the old nor new ogham years. It's the extra day within the old country saying, 'Wait for a year and a day.'

In the tradition of ogham divination, a mistletoe wand is cut and used in the same way as all the others.

To see mistletoe, set out at midwinter and journey to an ancient orchard, where the apple trees lean stripped of leaves, amid long wild grass. As the brass winter sun sends flame-rays from behind ice clouds, you see clumps of mistletoe, dark round shapes, embraced by the light, hanging like rotund crows' nests in the forks of each tree. You wonder at the intricacy of their many branched stems and massed gold and green foliage. Here and there white berries promise renewal. At the orchard's end, you find yourself gazing up at a venerable oak. High among its antlered top branches is the prize, a mistletoe clump, jealously embraced by the old forest guardian, leaves shining amber. A movement on a lower branch attracts your eye, and you see a robin gazing at you fearlessly from button eyes. He sings, sweet and brief, then hops away.

To choose the mistletoe in divination has a powerful effect. It brings health, fertility and success. It also demands respect. Just as mistletoe grows upon another tree, we're all intricately connected to all creation, so that whatever we do affects the whole. Mistletoe may bring fortune but with it comes responsibility, and the need to live a life that respects all other beings. It's also vital to accept that all fortune's within change, so change from any given state is inevitable.

Mistletoe, otherwise mystyldene or all-heal, is found in southern England and the Midlands. It grows on other trees, piercing their bark with its roots. A semi-parasite, it nourishes itself through its own leaves, as well as tapping its host's juices. Mistletoe is evergreen, but only grows on deciduous trees. Hawthorn, ash, lime and poplar are favourites, although crab apple and old apple trees are loved best. It occasionally grows on oak.

White berries appear mid-winter and contain a viscous fluid. Birds, spread mistletoe by eating the berries and then wiping their beaks on other trees. The missel thrush gained its name from this behaviour.

In herbalism, mistletoe is given to treat epilepsy and sterility. Although too much causes convulsions.

Roman author Pliny the Elder (23-79AD) recorded Gaulish Druids harvesting mistletoe. The harvesting took place on the 6th day of the Moon with a golden sickle, catching the plant in a white cloak. The ceremony was completed by the sacrifice of two white bulls. They used it as a drink to make any barren thing fertile, and as an antidote to all poisons.

Pliny suggested that the mistletoe symbolised the supreme being worshipped by the Druids. It was vitally important throughout all nations where oak cults predominated. The legendary Golden Bough of Nemi, that led Sir James Frazer to his anthropological breakthrough concerning the rites of sacred kingship, was mistletoe.

Frazer theorised that the Druids saw mistletoe as the spirit of the oak, containing it's spiritual essence and power. In the British oral tradition, the mistletoe symbolised the oak's phallus, and lopping it emasculated the divine king. After this, he would be ritually sacrificed, impaled by a mistletoe dart, and his flesh eaten. The heir to the throne would be passed the mistletoe bough, and initiated as king. The time of the divine king's sacrifice was the extra day, sacred to the mistletoe. Pliny's kinder Druids had replaced human sacrifice with an offering of bulls.

When the new king was handed the mistletoe, it gave him the right to wed the tribal goddess, who in the oak cult was the triple Moon goddess of a thousand names, which included: Diana, Danu, Anu, Ceridwen, Rhiannon and Jana. The mistletoe berry's the Full Moon.

Mistletoe folklore is still strong, and no Christmas is complete without it. It's still customary to kiss beneath hanging mistletoe. The more adventurous seize a sprig and go in pursuit of whoever they desire. Originally, a single berry was removed after each kiss, until the bough was bare, when it was considered to have lost its power. The plant is traditionally banned from churches as it's a pagan decoration.

Mistletoe provides powerful protection if worn or hung up, especially if gathered on Midsummer's Eve, the winter solstice or the 6th day of the Moon. Cut it with a gold or bronze implement and make sure it doesn't touch the ground.

If it's gathered for Christmas, a sprig left hanging until the next winter's bough is brought in, ensures that there'll be enough food in the house and protect it from lightning. Some say, 'Where mistletoe hangs, love will stay.' Others stuff it up their chimneys to stop evil spirits gaining access. It's also lucky to burn a sprig under the pancakes on Shrove Tuesday!

The bird that shares the extra day with mistletoe is that garden favourite, the robin (*Erithacus rubecula*), sometimes known as bobrobin, robinet or ruddock. The robin's poetic yet plaintive song, his friendliness and familiar red breast ensure he's as much a part of every enspirited garden as a fragrant rose bush.

To be kind to a robin brings great fortune, but to harm or kill one summons a terrible curse. If a robin taps at a window or enters the house, it omens a funeral within a year.

The British taboo on harming robins reminds that once they were sacred. Red always symbolises blood and life. The spirit of the summer god, slain at the summer solstice was believed to reside in the robin, until he returned reborn at the winter solstice, slew his rival and reigned again. The bird of the winter-god is the wren. The link between robins and the winter solstice is still displayed on Christmas cards and cakes. He's the hope of summer in the deeps of winter.

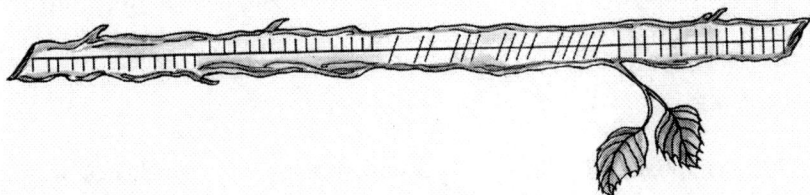

Chapter 23

Right Through the Forest

Summary of divinatory meanings:

Birch: new beginnings, inception, ideas, inspiration, reassessing past experiences, making plans, looking forwards, seeing the future forming through events and the actions of others, sweeping out the old, exorcism, accepting the way things have worked out, putting a part of life or experience firmly into the past and moving into the future, communication skills, sharing, prayer.

Rowan: quickening, attracting of positive influences, good fortune, well-being, fresh vigour, opportunities at present or about to arise, protection, secure environment, new projects, marvellous time for starting projects or a family, lucky for anything linked to land or animals, good will of the nature spirits.

Ash: an ally will step forward to assist or guide, moral support, protection of the gods, situations will arise that will turn things to your favour, sound resources, a helpmate, patron, relief from troubles, regaining control or strength, the need to keep striving, healing, attracting the required backing, a new friend.

Alder: inevitable change, transformation in accordance with Fate, sacrifice, something will alter and therefore be lost, sadness over what has fallen into the past, something fresh blossoming better than what has gone before, resurrection, cleansing by fire, the need to be flexible and accept evolution of circumstances, suffering if change is resisted.

Willow: grief, rejection by a lover, friend or family member, unrequited love, the need for realism concerning current relationships, have no illusions, split from a partner or lover, betrayal, enchantment, divination, secrets revealed, realisation of reality, sense of the sadness of the world and the inevitability of endings.

Blackthorn: strife, harsh conditions, opposing forces arising, the need to be strong and meet opponents and adversity head on, fight for your rights, refuse to compromise or give in, gaining strength from the weight of responsibilities to others whether family, partner or nation, malefic magic, an ill-wish, difficulties during pregnancy, reproductive troubles.

Hawthorn: a magical event, psychic or spiritual experience, deja vu, a stroke of luck, helping hand from the spirit world, a boost to healing after illness, renewed sense of purpose and well- being, unlucky to boast, warning not to enter a new love relationship or marriage, stay on chosen life- path, refuse to waste energies or diversify unnecessarily.

Oak: shelter, sanctuary, protection from life's storms, presence of enough strength and endurance to see things through, be firm, stay on course, current insecurity but the eventual return of security, continuation, preservation of and need to protect tradition, customs, family or nation, reassurance that justice will be done, opportunity for revenge.

Holly: a celebration, a gathering of friends or like-minded individuals, companionship, jollity, fun, an invitation, increase in social life and opportunities, teamwork promoted as a better option than individuality, team spirit, encouragement from others, working jointly towards mutual goals, a new friendship, a deepening of the bonds of friendship.

Hazel: pregnancy, news of a birth, starting a family, fertility, increase, a promising beginning, a new venture, positive trends, learning, success in study, innovatory ideas, inspiration from the Otherworld, the creation of great art, starting or working at anything in the correct spirit, promulgation of ideas, literacy, teaching.

Apple: a mystical experience, instinctive rapport with nature, a revelation, spiritual sustenance, reassurance, a hint of knowledge concerning the life beyond, awakening awareness of a vaster reality, support received from this source, communication with a spirit being, interaction with the faery kingdom, forging of a special bond with an animal or bird.

Blackberry/vine: joy, intoxication, exhilaration, getting carried away, unwise enthusiasm, the desire to convert everyone to a religion or interest, temptation, music, dance, the breaking down of personal and social barriers, an idea spreading, passion, a celebration or wild time, personal change through liberation, the need to channel energy wisely into creativity or promoting ideas.

Ivy: restrictions, progress slowing, feeling of hidden obstacles, being tied down, financial hardship, responsibilities to others standing in the way of personal desires, criticism, antagonism, people striving to restrict advancement or personal freedom, a relationship that takes away individual liberty, self-restriction, laziness, addiction, destructive relationship, lack of incentive.

Wheat Straw/Reed: established power, increase of responsibility, influence, authority, respect from others, strong role in the community, powers at their prime, the importance of consolidating position and maintaining authority, the need to be fair when wielding power and to achieve goals while things are positive.

Elder: something of importance soon to be revealed, knowledge or advice from others, the need to act wisely and respect the chances and pathway granted by the gods, a warning of changes on the way, preserve strength and halt any activity which could have negative consequences, insight, increase in wisdom and perception.

Scots pine/silver fir: emergence of a new spiritual path, turning point in the inner life, base decisions on higher perspectives, don't rely on anyone for advice or guidance. purity, transcendence, individuality, altruism, a healing time alone, retreat from the world, inner strength, celibacy, concentration on spirituality rather than relationships.

Gorse: passions peaking, sexual attraction, uncontrollable urges, affair, flirtation, dangerous liaison, fickleness, bond based on sex rather than emotion, promiscuity, prostitution, temptation, untidiness, sluttish behaviour, unruly antics, doubtful reputation or the danger of gaining one, losing respect, lack of self-control, new relationship fun but not lasting.

Heather: unsettling currents, insecurity, cycles of evolution transforming in ways not expected or planned for, new situations emerging, dispersion, dissemination, breaking up ground, a move of home or workplace due to circumstances, someone leaving home, friendship group or team going separate ways, adapt to any changes and see what opportunities they stimulate.

Aspen: emotional phase, reflection, mourning, nostalgia, memories, putting past events into perspective, acceptance, experiencing old emotions with new deeper awareness, bittersweet sensations, feelings of mortality and the inevitability of time and Fate, communion with the spirit realm, realisation that a particular life-phase is drawing to a close.

Yew: loss, bereavement, great change, end of a situation leading to new beginnings, a way is cleared for a fresh start, renewed sense of the eternity of all things, awareness of reincarnation, spirituality, mysticism, growing interest in magic or the occult.

Mistletoe: health, return to health, fertility, success, good fortune, a reminder of our responsibilities to others, the need to respect all other beings and see ourselves as part of a whole, an individual but also an integral part of a vast universe encompassing both spiritual and physical realities.

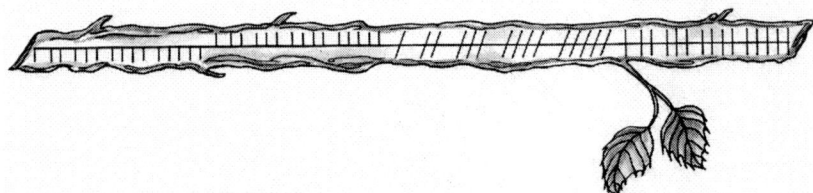

Chapter 24

The Ogham Calendar

Each ogham letter opens a door to the mysteries. Usually, an alphabet is a series of signs which represent the sounds of a given language. Anyone who's been taught which sounds correspond to which letters, can read a message written by anyone else in that language. This is the basis of written communication. In Britain today, we use the Latin alphabet, developed by the Romans.

In ogham, each letter signifies a sound, a divinatory meaning, a tree, bird, colour, and period of time. Originally there was probably a herb and animal too, but that knowledge has been lost.

The ogham letters are named after trees, and have a set sequence. Even before ogham became a written alphabet, this sequence of trees was used as a calendar, each tree representing a month, festival or season.

The peoples who originated ogham had no concept of a seven day week, or the Roman solar calendar of twelve months that we use now. To explore the original ogham calendar, we must enter a very strange world, that of the distant past, Britain during the Old Stone Age, a time after the end of the last Ice Age, but before the first plough had furrowed the earth. The tribes subsisted on meat, fish, shellfish, and wild growing roots, nuts, berries and fruit. These people were no different to us, just natives of another time, with different technologies, and brought up within a strong traditional tribal culture.

To follow the herds of deer from summer to winter feeding grounds, to predict the arrival of cod or salmon, or to be in the right place for the blackberry or nut harvests, it was vital to measure time accurately.

They measured time by six markers, sun, moon, day, night, summer and winter. Days and nights could be counted, allowing meetings to be planned and distances measured by an average day's march. From the beginning it was noted that the sun's journey through the sky grew longer each day until the summer solstice, and then declined until the winter solstice. The moon had two cycles: she waxed from New to Full Moon and then waned until the next New Moon, a period of around 29 or 29 $\frac{1}{2}$ days. The moon also rose in a different place each day, returning to her original position after 28 days.

Because the Moon goddess was the supreme deity, and the changes of her physical body in the night sky offered an easily visible time measure, the concept of a 'Moon', a lunar month was embraced, measured from one New Moon to the next. However, the lunar and solar years run independently of one another. There are sometimes twelve, other times thirteen New Moons between each winter solstice. These thirteen Moons were allotted to mythically important trees, chosen to reflect what was happening in nature during that Moon.

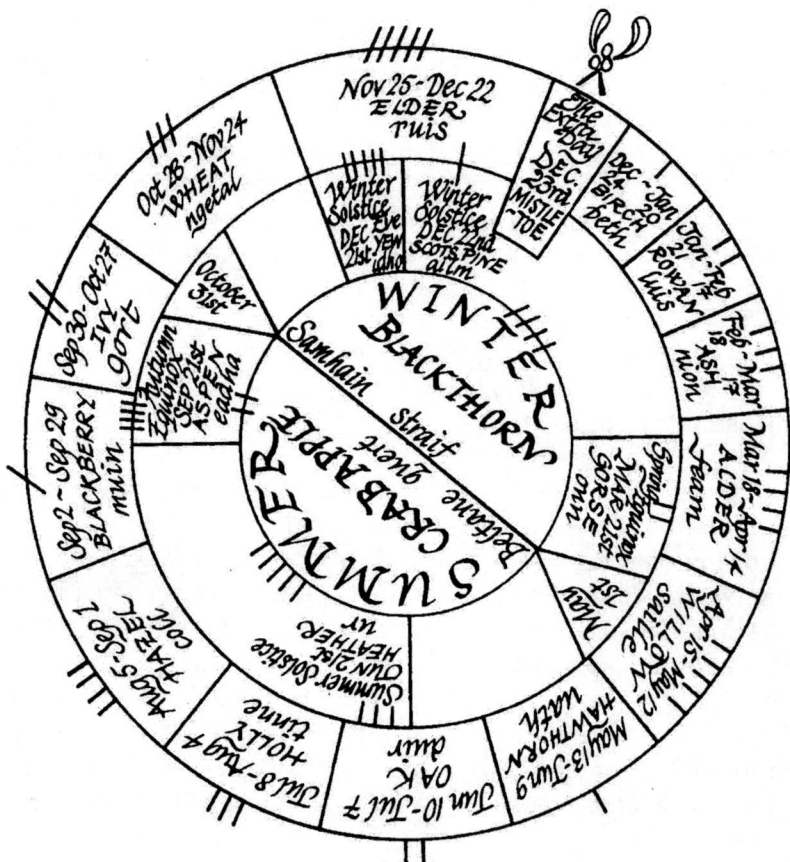

The OGHAM CALENDAR
The Wheel of the Year

Nov 25 - Dec 22 ELDER ruis

Oct 28 - Nov 24 WHEAT ngetal

Sep 30 - Oct 27 IVY gort

Sep 2 - Sep 29 BLACKBERRY muin

Aug 5 - Sep 1 HAZEL coll

Jul 8 - Aug 4 HOLLY tinne

Jun 10 - Jul 7 OAK duir

May 13 - Jun 9 HAWTHORN uath

Apr 15 - May 12 WILLOW saille

Mar 18 - Apr 14 ALDER fearn

Feb 18 - Mar 17 ASH nion

Jan 21 - Feb 17 ROWAN luis

Dec 24 - Jan 20 BIRCH beth

The Extra Day DEC. 23rd MISTLETOE

Winter Solstice DEC 21st Eve YEW idho

Winter Solstice DEC 22nd SCOTS PINE ailm

October 31st

Autumn Equinox SEP 21st ASPEN eadha

Summer Solstice JUN 21st HEATHER ur

May 1st

Spring Equinox MAR 21st GORSE onn

WINTER BLACKTHORN

SUMMER CRAB APPLE

Samhain straif

Beltane queirt

110

The lunar ogham year begins at the first New Moon after the winter solstice, December 21st.

Ogham lunar calendar for 2001:
Birch Moon, Dec 25th 2000 - birch bark as white as midwinter snow
Rowan Moon Jan 24th 2001 - bare of leaves the rowan awaits spring.
Ash Moon Feb 23rd - buds of new leaves begin to break.
Alder Moon 25th Mar - coming into full leaf the alder is reborn.
Willow Moon 23rd Apr - myriad catkins hang from the willow's branches.
Hawthorn Moon 23rd May - hawthorn blossom welcomes summer.
Oak Moon 21st Jun - the oak is in his summer glory.
Holly Moon 20th Jul - holly still evergreen even on the driest hottest days.
Hazel Moon 19th Aug - hazel nuts can be seen forming.
Blackberry Moon 17th Sep - blackberries ripen and become good to eat.
Ivy Moon 16th Oct - ivy is in full flower.
Elder Moon 15th Nov - the tree of the dark crone goddess, and deepest winter is her time.

The Reed Moon is inserted as the 12th Moon when an extra Moon's needed. The Elder Moon then becomes the 13th. This 'intercalary' Reed Moon's added when the Birch Moon would otherwise have begun before December 21st. It also ensures the tree for each Moon is seasonally correct.

Reed Moon October/November - a Moon ship adrift on winter waters.

Later, due to the variations in the occurrence of each Moon month from year to year, the old British priesthood, decided to make the ogham year entirely solar. This had the advantage that each month starts on the same day every year. To remember the Moon's sovereignty, thirteen 28 day months were decided on (see illustration).

The first day of the first month fell on the second day after the winter solstice, or to be exact, as darkness fell on the evening of December 23rd. Practically, we refer to the first day of the ogham year as December 24th. The ancient British began their days when the sun finally sank below the horizon. This was in honour of night's ruler, the moon. Modern convention begins days at 12.00pm exactly, allowing no flexibility for seasonal differences.

Thirteen ogham months of 28 days form a year of 364 days. One more day is needed to make the correct number, 365, for a complete solar year. This extra day is added on December 23rd. The thirteen month year survives in folklore, and the saying, 'a year and a day,' is still current. The 'day' refers to the 23rd, a day between years.

The reed was permanently granted the 12th month, and in some places became wheat. This happened after the introduction of agriculture and was linked to the sowing of winter cereals.

The next six ogham trees were linked to the five festivals of the solar year, and the 'extra' day that stands alone between years.

Gorse, March 21st spring equinox - flowers of fire herald spring.
Heather, June 21st summer solstice - royal purple blooms in the summer heat.
Aspen, Sep 21st autumn equinox - leaves glow amber before the fall.
Yew, Dec 21st winter solstice eve - evergreen yew promises rebirth.

Silver fir or scots pine, Dec 22nd winter solstice - pine torches to light the Longest Night.
Mistletoe, Dec 23rd, the extra day - a mistletoe dart to slay the king.

The remaining two ogham trees, crab apple and blackthorn, traditionally share months with hazel and willow, but they're primarily symbolic of the great seasonal polarities, summer and winter.

Crab apple, summer (beginning Beltane, May 1st) - pink blossom signs the season of sun.
Blackthorn, winter (beginning Samhain, October 31st) - dark purple sloes welcome winter cold.

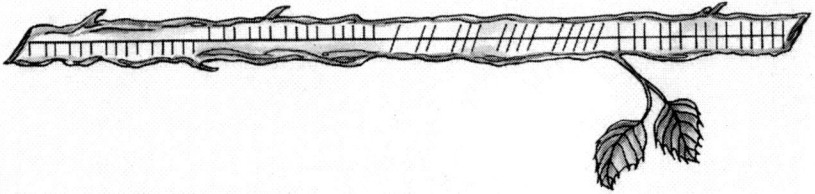

Chapter 25

Druídic Alphabets and Oghams

Ogham inscriptions grace stone monuments throughout the British Isles. Of 375 surviving, 316 are in Ireland. All are in a Celtic language, and mostly date from the 4th century AD. The mainland British inscriptions, have bilingual texts, reflecting both Latin and Celtic speaking population elements.

It's no coincidence that ogham, a new form of writing originating from among the indigenous Celts, began to appear on monuments in the 3rd century, just as the Roman Empire began to decline. For the British this fading, meant greater autonomy and a renaissance of native culture.

It's apparent to anyone studying ogham, that its characters are of the simplest form possible, just a series of dashes, designed for carving quickly and efficiently. The date of the inscriptions points to the fact that the ogham script was formulated quite late, by literate individuals who, while aware of Latin and Greek alphabets, chose not to use them.

The ogham script is more a cipher than an alphabet. To find the reasons for this we have to explore prehistory. Prior to the Roman conquest of Britain, the small nations that populated the country mostly spoke a language known as P-Celtic, whereas the majority of the Irish Celts, the Gaels, spoke Q-Celtic. Mainland Britain had other languages, now lost, but there was a loose national identity, and official business was all in Celtic. P-Celtic's the ancestor tongue of Cornish, Welsh and Breton.

Julius Caesar, who invaded Britain in 55BC, stated that the Gauls used Greek characters for writing. He was a highly educated man and would not have been mistaken. Most of the ancient world, from North Africa to Scandinavia, used Greek or Latin alphabets for business purposes, whatever hiero-glyphic or runic letters they used within their own culture.

By the time of the Emperor Claudius' successful invasion of Britain, 43AD, British kings such as Caractacus and Togodumnus, were richer and more powerful. Although mostly hostile to Rome, they had increased trading links with the Empire, and were adopting Roman fashions and lifestyle, to the extent of using Latin inscriptions on their coinage.

British culture: poetry, religion, genealogy, mythology, history and art, was preserved orally, passed by word of mouth, from generation to generation. The Britons also had a caste of priests, the druids, who were intertribal, exercising influence over the rulers of the various British nations. The druids were more than a priesthood, their jurisdiction included: law, education, science, the arts and the calendar. Luckily, druidic learning was also strictly oral, everything being committed to memory. As long as one druid/druidess survived, their

Druidic & Ancient Alphabets

r g m c t s f n l b

a o u e i

beth-luis-nion

knowledge stayed intact.

When the Romans arrived, druidic power was waning. It was strong among the indigenous inland British, Welsh, Cornish and Scottish tribes, but the Belgic nations that had crossed over from Gaul and conquered Southern England, although P-Celtic speaking, were ruled by vigorous modernising kings, who sought to cast off what they saw as the restrictive influence of druidism.

The Romans recognised that the druids, as keepers of the British cultural flame, had potential for invoking patriotism and revolt against their rule. They strove to destroy the cult, making a point of erasing the druid stronghold at Anglesey.

Ultimately, the Romans failed. The druids weren't just career-priests. Any Briton who wanted a child educated would send them to a druidic college, where they would be initiated into the druidic cult. This meant that the entire Celtic aristocracy and educated classes were to some extent druids. They just vanished back into the general population and preserved their knowledge until Roman power faded.

After Rome fell, the new British rulers went back to their ancestral ways, but recognising that they were now living in a highly literate world, they wanted their own way of writing. Ogham was invented, but behind the series of dashes we know as ogham, was a true script of distinctive characters. This, which we'll refer to as the 'beth-luis-nion,' or 'b-l-n,' had existed from earliest times, but was kept secret by the druids, and used solely for divination and magic. Ogham was a compromise, a unique script with the same phonetic values as the original b-l-n, each character representing one of its letters. Ogham meant that the Celtic languages could be written in a Celtic script, without the true b-l-n characters falling into unworthy hands, and losing magical validity.

bobileth

j e u o a r g c m d n s f l l s

aleph beth gimel daleth he waw zayin heth teth yod kaph lamed

mem nun samekh ayin pe tsadhe qoph resh shin taw

Phoenician
circa 8th century B.C.

Comparing the Alphabets

Modern Roman	b	l	n	f	s	a	t	c	m
beth-luis-nion									
bobileth									
Phoenician									

Modern Roman	g	p	r	a	o	u	e	i/j
beth-luis-nion								
bobileth								
Phoenician								

Phoenician waw 'Y' developed into 'f' and 'u'

other likenesses:- bobileth 'j' and Phoenician 'samekh' ‡

119

The magical beth-luis-nion script survived, and leaked into the public arena in the early 20th century. It survives in two forms, the 'beth-luis-nion,' preserving the original 'b-l-n' letter order, and the 'bobileth' recording the later 'b-l-f' sequence.

It may seem incredible that an alphabet survived unrecorded for two or more thousand years, but it's possible. Studying the two scripts, it's evident that they share the same origin, but were perhaps developed separately. The letter 'P' finds a place in the beth-luis-nion, replacing ogham's 'ng.' This suggests that this version of the script was preserved by P-Celtic speakers. The letters 'q/cc, ss/z or h.,' are not represented. These have either been kept secret or are lost knowledge.

Fascinatingly, studying old alphabets, it can be seen that there are close parallels between ancient Phoenician and b-l-n/b-l-f. Even the strange b-l-n vowels are similar to their Phoenician equivalents. The Phoenicians, the Canaanites of the Bible, are credited with the invention of the phonetic alphabet, circa the 15th century BC. From this source, Hebrew, Arabic, Greek, Latin and Runic etc, all descend.

The Phoenician script consists of 22 letters, all consonants. The Greeks adopted it in the 9th century BC and adapted it to their own language by changing some of the phonetic values to vowel sounds.

Folklore has long held that Phoenician traders sailed to Britain and settled, influencing British culture. Although they may have come via Greece, the b-l-n/b-l-f letters are close enough to Phoenician to have been derived directly from that source. The druids too, had to convert some of the consonants to vowels, because of the extreme importance of these sounds, 'the breaths,' in Celtic language and myth. The letter order was also changed for mythical, mystical and calendrical reasons.

The relevance of the beth-luis-nion and the bobileth today, is that they can be carved on wooden wands, slats or discs, for use in divination. They offer more easily recognised characters to represent the ogham trees. Use your imagination to recreate the missing letters, or adapt other Phoenician characters.

Whether the b-l-n and b-l-f are druidic relics or an invention of a 13th or 20th century bard, the real test is whether they work.

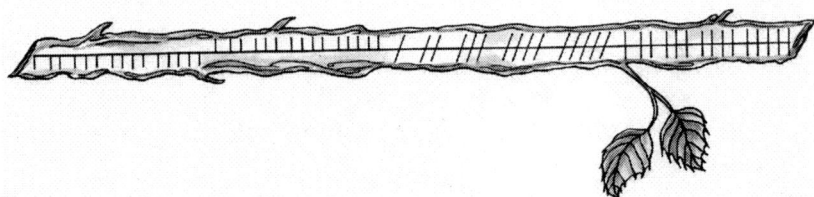

Chapter 26

The Druids - Facts and Folklore

During our journey through the ogham alphabet and calendar, the druids have cropped up numerous times. They're intimately connected in both myth and fact, with Celtic traditions and spirituality.

It's safe to say that more tosh has been written about them, than about almost anything else. They have been made the playthings and propagandists of every cause that's needed some ancient magical back up. Historians such as William Stukely promoted them as a patriarchal Levite priesthood, worshipping in true Old Testament style. Some saw them as Phoenician travellers who civilised the cavemen of Britain, teaching them to build megalithic monuments. Other writers strove to prove that the Celts were a lost tribe of Israel. Later, the druids became icons of Welsh nationalism, credited as the source of all Cymric and Cornish culture. Even British Prime Minister, Lloyd George was an initiated 'druid.'

In the 1960's, the hippies championed druidism as an environmentally friendly alternative spirituality, and began holding festivals, such as the now defunct Stonehenge event, at Neolithic sites. The white robed druids still seen on television celebrating the summer solstice, are mostly inheritors of traditions begun in Victorian times, although many claim roots stretching back to Celtic pre-history.

The problem is that druidic learning was entirely oral, and can therefore be worked up from the surviving evidence: accounts by Roman and Greek authors, archaeology and folklore, into any shape that takes an author's fancy. As the anomalist and scientific researcher Charles Forte allegedly once said, 'For every expert, there is an equal and opposite expert.'

From the Classical authors, especially, Julius Caesar, Diodorus Siculus and Tacitus, we do know a fair amount about Celtic society and the druids. For details read Julius Caesar's *Gallic War* and Tacitus' *The Agricola and the Germania.*

It seems the druids were an intertribal priesthood, whose influence was pervasive wherever the Celts had settled. They ran the universities and preserved all knowledge: arts, sciences, divination, spirituality, agriculture and crafts. Another main role was as legislators and judges, and as peacemakers, settling feuds and calming war situations between tribes.

Their power was damaged by Rome, who saw them as a political threat and balked at their continuing use of human sacrifice. The conversion of the Roman Empire to Christianity helped the process, driving any druidic survivals underground, to be preserved as old wives' tales, and in the witch-cults of the formerly Celtic nations.

Folklore is filled with druid-lore. I have uncritically set down all the traditions I can remember. Some are recorded in works on folklore, others passed along by word of mouth.

The oldest name of Britain was Albion. Along with Ireland, then known as Ierne, and the other offshore islands, it was regarded as sacred and the centre of all druidism. The druids were an institution of the aboriginal inhabitants of Britain, France and Germany, and were adopted by the Celts on their arrival, probably beginning 800BC.

Druidism was the second religion of the British Isles. The first was witchcraft, which can be defined as mankind's oldest belief system, and centred around the clan wise-woman or man. This dates from the genesis of humanity. Druidism began in the first millennium BC, as a response to social change, growing population, the immigration of the first Celtic tribes, a need for some form of national rather than tribal cohesion, and a shift from matriarchy to patriarchy. The third religion of Britain was Christianity.

The druids used stone circles and megalithic monuments for worship, also holy wells, tors, natural rock formations, small islands and sacred groves. Their rites involved human and animal sacrifice. One occasion when this was practised, was to protect the foundation of a standing stone, road, temple or dwelling.

They were magicians and could raise storms and deep mists. Some Druids practised divination, by scrying, astrology, casting wooden wands (oghams), communication with the spirits of the dead and observation of animals, birds, insects and weather formations. They had the power to cast glamours: illusions of vast armies, demons, fire or phantom ships, sometimes causing trees or standing stones to come to life and walk.

Old sacred sights and druidic relics, are protected by curses and spirit guardians placed by druid invocations. The entire island of Britain is enveloped by a druidic spell, protecting it from invasion. On the eve of any war, the spirit guardians of Albion will be seen out at sea, atop hillforts or gathering by tombs and stone circles. Druids could 'lay' or exorcise ghosts, as well as 'set' them to cause a haunting.

There were female as well as male druids. Old druid knowledge is kept and passed down within certain families to this day.

The druids' sacred tree was the oak, plant - mistletoe, herbs - vervain, trefoil and hyssop, birds - wren, goose, cockerel and raven, animals - bull, stag, ram, horse and hare. If a plant was collected for magical purposes, it was gathered on the sixth day of the moon, and not allowed to touch the ground.

The druid festivals were the winter solstice (December 22nd), Imbolc (February 2nd), Spring Equinox (March 21st), Beltane (May 1st), Summer Solstice (June 21st), Lughnasad (August 1st), Autumn Equinox (September 22nd) and Samhain (October 31st). There were other local festivals in honour of local gods.

The druids taught reincarnation, and that there was no escaping the consequences of any action, which could follow you into the next life. Consequences are seen as part and parcel of an action, not separate from it. Their justice was harsh, 'An eye for an eye,' etc but always fair and compassionate. The human sacrifices burnt in huge wicker baskets or otherwise disposed of, were criminals, either sentenced to such an end, or who had chosen it to clean themselves of their crimes and propitiate the gods. All animals, trees, rivers, oceans, standing stones and places have souls, but humans do not reincarnate as animals.

The chief British and druidic deities, were an omnipotent Triple Moon, Mother and harvest goddess, in one form called Sulis, Nodens, a healing and prophetic god, Taranus, a thunder deity, Cocidius, a war god, and antler horned Cernunnos, who equates partly with Mercury. Epona the horse goddess, another form of the Great Mother, was also popular. Gods and goddesses had almost as many names as there were tribes, and there were numerous local gods and goddesses too.

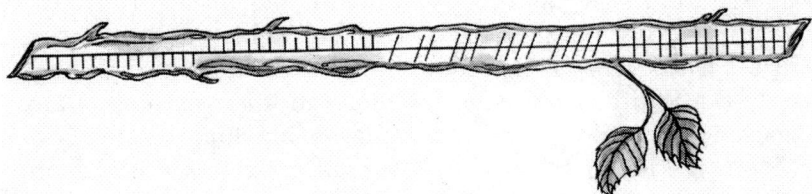

Chapter 27

Prophetic Queens and Sacred Kings

In this chapter it's hoped to answer such important questions as: 'Why are ravens kept at the Tower of London?' 'Did Celtic warriors really share their women?' and, 'Why vicars wear dresses at the altar?'

In these pages, 'sacred kings' have been referred to a number of times, a subject vital to the understanding of ancient religion.

It's worth reminding the reader, that Clio the muse of history, inspires historians in different ways, and worse still, some historians refuse her advances and seek to expound their own dry-as-dust theories, removing the magic and poetry from the past. So, we'll invoke Clio with an age old spell, 'Once upon a time ...'

In Britain, in the Golden Age, when no plough had raped the earth, the first people lived by hunting, fishing and gathering forest fruits. They called themselves Albions, and worshipped only the White Goddess, the Moon, and knew nothing of any gods. She was revered in three phases, blushing Maiden New Moon, fickle, flirtatious and romantic, Mother Full Moon, sensual, sexual, fertile, childbearing and nurturing, and Grandmother Dark Moon, sorcerous, death dealing, cannibalistic, and prophetic.

A tribe's high priestess represented her and was Queen, the goddess' voice on earth. She ruled all matters, temporal and spiritual, holding court in sacred groves, or on island shrines like the Thames' islands, or from caves such as Wookey Hole in Somerset. The priestess was surrounded by a college of women and girls devoted to the goddess' service, chosen for their gifts in art, magic or divination, or their physical perfection. The mysteries and culture of the tribe were preserved and taught orally from within this college. A Queen's territory varied from the size of a modern parish, to vast hunting grounds.

Society was matriarchal, clans traced descent through the mother, and fatherhood was not a recognised concept. It was assumed that women were impregnated by spirits within the wind, sacred fire, waters or certain foods. Sex was a recreational or sacred act, and marriage an unknown custom.

When Julius Caesar in his 'Gallic Wars,' stated of the Britons, 'Wives are shared between groups of ten or twelve men ... ' he was referring sarcastically to survivals of matriarchal sexual freedom.

It's likely that the non-recognition of the father's role was a political denial, rather like the British government's pre-2000 failure to recognise global warming.

The tribes lived split into clans, extended families, descending from a common female ancestor. The clans would meet up for festivals. Those at Beltane, Midsummer and Midwinter were orgiastic, with the resulting children adopted into the mother's clan, or in the case of the priestesses, kept within the college. At puberty, males would be fostered out to a suitable clan.

Clans would be named after an indigenous species of animal, bird or insect, and derive their ritual, magic and customs from its behaviour. The fox, wolf, bear, deer, horse, buffalo, crow, robin, heron and wren were all clan animals. Traces of this remain in British surnames: 'Watt,' 'Watkins' are from the hare (watt), 'Fox,' 'Tod,' from the fox (tod).

Fatherhood was eventually recognised because of pressure from immigrants, Celtic and otherwise, coming to Britain. Male status improved accordingly. The ruling priestess would choose a male consort, usually after gruelling combats or tests of strength. He would be revered for a year, and then at the due season, sacrificed, and his blood sprinkled across the land to ensure the fertility of trees and beasts.

Human sacrifice is only unacceptable from 21st century cultural standpoints. Many people now balk at the concept of being killed in battle, sacrificing oneself for one's country, yet within the last hundred years, millions of British and Commonwealth soldiers did so, unhesitatingly. In a religious sense, the sacred king made the same sacrifice, believing thoroughly that in return for his giving his life, the earth would yield and give sustenance to his people. After death his bones or skull would be transported to a funerary isle, and kept there to serve as an oracle.

The king was periodically allowed to deputise for the priestess, taking responsibility for some of her religious duties. In some cultures, he was only allowed to do this if he wore female clothes. Christian priests adopted their dress from the pagan Roman priests, inheriting a tradition that emanates from earlier matriarchal times. That's why Church of England clergy wear dresses.

As other peoples settled Britain, especially the Celtic tribes, circa 800BC, peace was often made by marrying the male gods of the incomers to the goddess of the aboriginals. The sacred king became a representative of the new god.

The incomers were stronger militarily and the kings gained in power. The new druidic priesthood began to usurp the prerogatives of the Moon goddess and her priestesses. By the time the Belgic Celts came from the continent around 200BC, most Celtic tribes were patriarchal, descent being traced through the male line, and their kings were not required to be sacrificed. Instead it was done symbolically, with criminals, prisoners of war, or animals slain in their place. Although it's remembered in folklore, the sacrifice of kings was banned by the conquering Romans, who had learned to abhor it, although they themselves had formerly done the same.

Later sacred kings were gods incarnate, but earlier ones were embodiments of tribal or clan totems. Some were originally seen as tree spirits, oak, ash or alder kings, especially before agriculture, when acorns or samara, the fruit of the ash were staples of diet. The ogham tree alphabet preserves the tale of the sacred king's mythical and ritual life through the course of a year.

The Celtic deity Bran, was linked to the alder and the raven. His sacred birds were kept at his temples. When Bran's earthly incarnation was sacrificed, his spirit was believed to take residence in one of the temple birds, and inspire the resident priestess to prophecy. The Tower of London on White Hill was formerly the sight of a temple dedicated to Bran, hence the myth of his head being buried there. In fact, it's where all the sacred kings titled 'Bran' had their decapitated and pickled heads interred.

Bran's sacred ravens are still kept at the Tower of London, ostensibly because of a belief that if they leave, Britain will fall. The British royal family have ancestors going back to 'Bran,' and each successive monarch has preserved the sacred ravens.

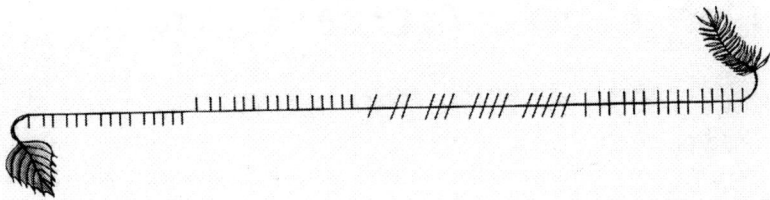

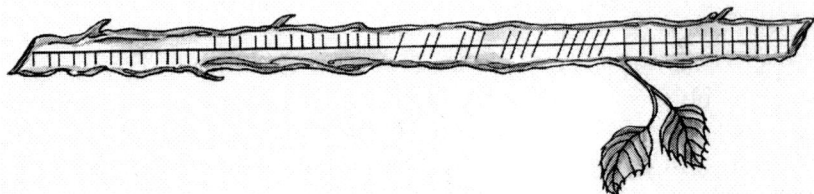

Chapter 28

The God of the Year

As we've seen, the ancient matriarchal religious system was based on the worship of the omnipotent Moon goddess. As the male gender began to demand spiritual recognition, the concept of a 'sacred king' rose to prominence. He was always a man in his prime, chosen as consort by a tribe's priestess-queen, the earthly representative of the Moon goddess. He was king for a year before being sacrificed and replaced. This enforced yearly 'life,' was a mirror of the mythical life of the god of the year, who was believed to be incarnate within the sacred king.

The beth-luis-nion sequence of trees, acts as a calendar that records this mythical and ritual year. The details varied, according to place, date and tribe, but the essence remained:

> Birch: Dec 24th-Jan 20th - first days, the god is reborn with the sun, a babe, purified and free of the past. The sacred king is of course an adult, but he's kept hidden, and is referred to as 'newborn.'

Rowan: Jan 21st-Feb 17th - the time of quickening, the god-child grows swiftly. Rowan's month contains the Imbolc festival, now February 2nd, the feast of lights, when the god-child is led in procession before the public for the first time. During the mysteries of the feast, he's named and blessed. The next morning his mother takes him down to the sacred river, places him in a coracle and sets him adrift to float where Fate wills.

Ash: Feb 18th-March 17th - the child is found washed up on the banks of a sacred island by an old priestess, the goddess in crone-guise. She befriends and cares for him, devoting herself to his needs. Although a male child, before puberty he's considered a 'girl,' dresses the part and lives among the priestesses.

Alder: Mar 18th-Apr 14th - on the sacred isle where kings are laid to rest, by the thick alder groves, he grows to the end of his childhood and the start of maturity. He's initiated into the Goddess' mysteries at the spring equinox March 21st, symbolically dies, throwing off his child-life, and is reborn a man.

Willow: Apr 15th-May 12th - the god's foster-mother prophesies his future for him. He accepts his Destiny and parts tearfully from her, crossing the waters to return to his own people. The Beltane feast, now May 1st links within this month, although as it's a lunar festival, it can occur later.

The god is in his sexual and physical prime at Beltane. This feast of summer's start with its leaping fires, outdoor gatherings and sexual promiscuity, welcomes the god back to his tribe. He is ritually married to the priestess-queen, playing the role of goddess in Maiden phase.

This is remembered in folklore's woodland marriage of the May King and Queen. In matriarchal times, in the following celebration, the sacred king would impregnate as many of the young women as possible.

Hawthorn: May 13th-June 9th - a time of rest after Beltane's excesses, for communication with the spirit-worlds and divination. Nature's growing, as are the wild children of the animals and birds, and the human babies begun at the festival.

Oak: Jun 10th-Jul 7th - the god is at his peak, ruling a flourishing natural kingdom. This is celebrated at the summer solstice fire-feast, June 21st, another joining of this reality with the Hidden-world.

Holly: Jul 8th-Aug 4th - a time of gatherings and jollity, the first fruits and crops are harvested. The feast of Lughnasad takes place August 1st, when thanks are given for the gifts of the Earth Mother. The festival has a bittersweet touch. Beneath the celebrations and athletic contests there's a darker purpose. The tribe's young men compete in strength and speed, the winner's crowned with oak leaves. Secretly the priestess-queen is choosing the next sacred king, marking him out for crowning after the ritual sacrifice of the present incumbent.

Hazel: Aug 5th-Sep 1st - the tribe has abundant food as harvest continues. In these days of plenty there's time for culture, art, poetry, and religion. The mysteries of the Goddess are celebrated and taught.

Blackberry Sep 2nd-Sep 29th - the autumn equinox and Harvest Moon herald summer's end. Harvest festival's celebrated, along with the making of the first beer, ale or cider, and the gathering of hazel nuts. All of these celebrations had a licentious character in pagan times, which has continued in varying forms until today.

Ivy: Sep 30th-Oct 27th - the winter Crone-goddess begins to bind summer in her grasp, as the ivy binds the virile holly, sapping nature's energies.

Wheat: Oct 28th-Nov 24th - the god-king's powers are waning as winter grows. The festival of Samhain takes place, on the night of October 31st. This is a feast of spirits, the true beginning of the winter half-year. During it the king's death is prophesied, and a hag-like priestess gifts him an apple - a badge of his imminent journey to the Otherworld.

Elder: Nov 25th-Dec 22nd - the winter witch-mother now rules nature, a barren wasteland - the god-king's old and dying, no longer able to keep the world fertile. The last days of his reign are celebrated with misrule and revelry, culminating at the winter solstice itself, 22nd December, last day of the ogham year.

The day of the ailing king's sacrifice was originally December 23rd, the extra day that stands beyond the old year, and before the new. The priestess-queen lures him to a place by water, that's neither wet land nor dry, where his replacement, the king in waiting is concealed. He dies a fivefold death, lamed, shot by an arrow or pierced by a spear, crucified, then decapitated, and torn apart by the priestesses and eaten raw. The heart or liver would go to the new king. Scraps of him were then handed out among the tribespeople as an act of communion. His flesh and blood were the 'life,' the vigour and fertility of nature.

His decapitated head was preserved by smoking or pickling, then ferried across to one of the many

'Avalons,' the sacred burial islands, where it would be kept in one of the goddess' shrines as an oracle. His soul was believed to live on in one of the temple ravens, or sometimes an adder.

The king dies at the end of the sacred thirteenth month, that of the elder - one explanation why some consider thirteen unlucky.

The god is born again on the 24th, reincarnated in the body of another sacred king, and another year begins.

This cycle, based on the solar calendar, superseded an earlier, solely lunar one, in which each month was a full moon cycle, lasting from one New Moon, to the day before the next. The old lunar calendar ran: Birch, Rowan, Ash, Alder, Willow, Hawthorn, Oak, Holly, Hazel, Blackberry, Ivy, Elder. Usually there's twelve Moons between the solstices. On occasions a thirteenth's needed to bring the calendar back into line with the seasons. This extra Moon was the Reed Moon, added between the Ivy and Elder Moons.

The sacred king was ritually or literally sacrificed at the Full Elder Moon. The reality of human/king sacrifice within many cultures, was thought to have been proved satisfactorily by Sir James G. Frazer, in his seminal work, 'The Golden Bough.' However, the debate has been opened again. Regardless of academia, the concept's still alive within folklore, recorded historically in 'mock' mayor and 'boy bishop' customs, as well as in stories about the 'assassination' of England's King Rufus in the New Forest, and St. George's dramatic death and rebirth.

Mythically, the story of an omnipotent goddess and her son/lover is represented in most legend cycles, from Isis and Osiris, through Ishtar and Tammuz, Aphrodite and Adonis, to Semele and Dionysus.

It may be hard in the 21st century to visualise a male in his prime, voluntarily electing to die as the symbol of a god/nature spirit. In matriarchal times, the outlook was different. Reincarnation into a paradise realm or an exalted state on earth was promised. Without technology lives were shorter, and on witnessing uncomfortable old age and untreatable illness in others, it may have seemed a good option to be slain in glory at the peak of health. Also, the sacred king and his society believed that his sacrifice was necessary to renew nature, and the wellbeing and fertility of the tribe. Politically it allowed the Priestess-queen to retain power, as the yearly king did not have time to rebel against her. It also cut down on the number of potentially trouble making males.

As matriarchy waned and kings gained more real power, the sacrifice tradition faded. The king stayed on, at first living only for the Great Lunar year of eight years, when lunar and solar cycles coincide, then for the Greater Lunar Year of 19 years, when the two cycles coincide more exactly.

Later still, substitute sacrifices were made in the king's place: a younger brother, child, twin brother, a 'mock' king, usually a lad or criminal raised to kingship for just one day, an animal totem, or even an artificial effigy. By the time patriarchy was established, kings lived until they fell in battle or from old age, and the sacrifice was of animals or wholly symbolic, a ritual drama as exampled by the English Mumming plays, where Saint or King George is slain by the Turkish night, a man with his face blacked.

The 'black' man symbolises another part of the sacred king's legend. In some cultures there was a summer king, who ruled the bright year-half between the winter solstice and the summer solstice, and a winter king, who lorded it over the dark year-half, between the summer solstice and the winter solstice. The 'Turkish' Knight is the winter lord slaying his summer counterpart at Midsummer. His blacked face echoes the long nights and shadows of winter.

These two adversarial gods are also remembered in folklore and myth: King Arthur's rival was dark Mordred, Romulus fought Remus, Lleu's (Lugh) challenger was Goronwy. Even Odin was seasonally displaced form his throne by the winter god Uller.

The 'dark' Lord symbolises the bareness of the winter wasteland, nature lying dormant beneath the snows. This juxtaposition of the two seasonal gods is strangely reflected in Christian tradition, in which the summer solstice has become June 24th's Johnsmas, celebrating the nativity of St. John the Baptist, who gave way before Christ, while December 25th is Christmas, the nativity of Jesus.

Early British tradition remembers the seasonal gods as the summer oak-king, and winter holly-king. In the ogham calendar, the Oak month's June 10th-July 7th. The 7th ends the oak/summer year-half, which began with the first ogham month, Birch, on December 24th. The Holly month runs July 8th-August 4th. The 8th begins the holly/winter year-half.

One reason why 7 is a lucky number, is that the summer-king was sacrificed, usually by beheading at the summer solstice in the seventh month.

In the British Isles, the slaying of the two gods came to be celebrated at slightly different times. The old feast of Lughnasad, August 1st, later the Christian festival of Lammas, was the time when the first fruits of the fields and trees were offered to the gods, and thanks given. As a start-of-harvest feast, it marked summer's fertile height. It was also associated with athletic competitions. Oral tradition knows it as 'Mourning for Lugh,' the festival at which Lugh, the summer spirit, is sacrificed by his rival god. The games were held first, that a suitable Dark Lord could be chosen from among the young men.

The ritual end of the Dark Lord, was transferred to December 26th, Boxing Day. Possibly under early Christian influence, December 25th was thought to mark the actual winter solstice, therefore making the 26th, the 'extra' sacred day which stood beyond the end of the old year, and before the beginning of the new.

Boxing Day was otherwise known as St. Stephen's Day. Folklore and custom remembers it's ancient ceremonial nature in unusual ways. It's an old country custom to go hunting on Boxing Day, and in some places, that blood has to be shed before the hunter can return home, whether the victim's a small bird or squirrel.

Boxing day's also the day of the Wren Hunt, when village boys and men scour the hedgerows seeking this diminutive bird. Sometimes he's killed and paraded around the locality crucified. In kinder districts he's carried with royal pomp in a decorated cage and released afterwards. There's always songs and hijinks, and the 'wren boys' are often in fancy dress. They go from door to door, singing a special 'wren song' and displaying their victim. It's lucky for householders to donate money to their cause.

This custom was widespread in England, Wales, the Isle of Man, and parts of Ireland, and Scotland. The wren is the 'king' of winter, superseded by his rival, the sun-chested robin, who still stands triumphant on our Christmas cards.

Bibliography

Major Sources

The White Goddess, Robert Graves (Faber & Faber Ltd 1948)

The Greek Myths, Robert Graves (Penguin Books Ltd 1955)

The Golden Bough, Sir James G. Frazer (MacMillan & Co Ltd 1922)

The Fairies in Tradition and Literature, Katherine Briggs (Routledge & Kegan Paul Ltd 1967)

Somerset Folklore, Ruth Tongue (The Folklore Society 1965)

Somerset Cider - Customs and Folklore, Jon Dathen (The Watchet Press 2001)

Country Customs, Ralph Whitlock (B. T. Batsford Ltd 1978)

A Dictionary of British Folk Customs, Christina Hole (Helicon Publishing Ltd 1976)

The English Festivals, Laurence Whistler (William Heinemann Ltd 1947)

Old English Customs and Ceremonials, F. J. Drake-Carnell (Charles Scribner's Sons 1938)

A Dictionary of Plant-Lore, Roy Vickery (Oxford University Press 1995)

Trees and Shrubs of Britain (Readers Digest Association Ltd 1981)

Our Woodlands, Heaths and Hedges, W. S. Coleman (George Routledge & Sons Ltd 1907)

Birds of Britain (Readers Digest Association Ltd 1981)

British Nesting Birds, W. Percival Westell (J. M. Dent & Sons Ltd 1910)

Julius Caesar's, 'The Conquest of Gaul,' Trans S. A. Handford (Penguin Books 1951)

Tacitus', 'The Agricola and the Germania,' Trans S. A. Handford (Penguin Books 1948)

And very special thanks to everyone who gave verbal testimonials, on trees, birds, countrylore, magic and mysteries.

FREE DETAILED CATALOGUE

Capall Bann is owned and run by people actively involved in many of the areas in which we publish. A detailed illustrated catalogue is available on request, SAE or International Postal Coupon appreciated. **Titles can be ordered direct from Capall Bann, post free in the UK** (cheque or PO with order) or from good bookshops and specialist outlets.

Do contact us for details on the latest releases at: **Capall Bann Publishing, Auton Farm, Milverton, Somerset, TA4 1NE.** Titles include:

A Breath Behind Time, Terri Hector
Angels and Goddesses - Celtic Christianity & Paganism, M. Howard
Arthur - The Legend Unveiled, C Johnson & E Lung
Astrology The Inner Eye - A Guide in Everyday Language, E Smith
Auguries and Omens - The Magical Lore of Birds, Yvonne Aburrow
Asyniur - Womens Mysteries in the Northern Tradition, S McGrath
Beginnings - Geomancy, Builder's Rites & Electional Astrology in the
      European Tradition, Nigel Pennick
Between Earth and Sky, Julia Day
Book of the Veil , Peter Paddon
Caer Sidhe - Celtic Astrology and Astronomy, Vol 1, Michael Bayley
Caer Sidhe - Celtic Astrology and Astronomy, Vol 2 M Bayley
Call of the Horned Piper, Nigel Jackson
Cat's Company, Ann Walker
Celtic Faery Shamanism, Catrin James
Celtic Faery Shamanism - The Wisdom of the Otherworld, Catrin James
Celtic Lore & Druidic Ritual, Rhiannon Ryall
Celtic Sacrifice - Pre Christian Ritual & Religion, Marion Pearce
Celtic Saints and the Glastonbury Zodiac, Mary Caine
Circle and the Square, Jack Gale
Compleat Vampyre - The Vampyre Shaman, Nigel Jackson
Creating Form From the Mist - The Wisdom of Women in Celtic Myth and
      Culture, Lynne Sinclair-Wood
Crystal Clear - A Guide to Quartz Crystal, Jennifer Dent
Crystal Doorways, Simon & Sue Lilly
Crossing the Borderlines - Guising, Masking & Ritual Animal Disguise in the
      European Tradition, Nigel Pennick
Dragons of the West, Nigel Pennick
Earth Dance - A Year of Pagan Rituals, Jan Brodie
Earth Harmony - Places of Power, Holiness & Healing, Nigel Pennick
Earth Magic, Margaret McArthur

Eildon Tree (The) Romany Language & Lore, Michael Hoadley
Enchanted Forest - The Magical Lore of Trees, Yvonne Aburrow
Eternal Priestess, Sage Weston
Eternally Yours Faithfully, Roy Radford & Evelyn Gregory
Everything You Always Wanted To Know About Your Body, But So Far
    Nobody's Been Able To Tell You, Chris Thomas & D Baker
Face of the Deep - Healing Body & Soul, Penny Allen
Fairies in the Irish Tradition, Molly Gowen
Familiars - Animal Powers of Britain, Anna Franklin
Fool's First Steps, (The) Chris Thomas
Forest Paths - Tree Divination, Brian Harrison, Ill. S. Rouse
From Past to Future Life, Dr Roger Webber
Gardening For Wildlife Ron Wilson
God Year, The, Nigel Pennick & Helen Field
Goddess on the Cross, Dr George Young
Goddess Year, The, Nigel Pennick & Helen Field
Goddesses, Guardians & Groves, Jack Gale
Handbook For Pagan Healers, Liz Joan
Handbook of Fairies, Ronan Coghlan
Healing Book, The, Chris Thomas and Diane Baker
Healing Homes, Jennifer Dent
Healing Journeys, Paul Williamson
Healing Stones, Sue Philips
Herb Craft - Shamanic & Ritual Use of Herbs, Lavender & Franklin
Hidden Heritage - Exploring Ancient Essex, Terry Johnson
Hub of the Wheel, Skytoucher
In Search of Herne the Hunter, Eric Fitch
Inner Celtia, Alan Richardson & David Annwn
Inner Mysteries of the Goths, Nigel Pennick
Inner Space Workbook - Develop Thru Tarot, C Summers & J Vayne
Intuitive Journey, Ann Walker Isis - African Queen, Akkadia Ford
Journey Home, The, Chris Thomas
Kecks, Keddles & Kesh - Celtic Lang & The Cog Almanac, Bayley
Language of the Psycards, Berenice
Legend of Robin Hood, The, Richard Rutherford-Moore
Lid Off the Cauldron, Patricia Crowther
Light From the Shadows - Modern Traditional Witchcraft, Gwyn
Living Tarot, Ann Walker
Lore of the Sacred Horse, Marion Davies
Lost Lands & Sunken Cities (2nd ed.), Nigel Pennick
Magic of Herbs - A Complete Home Herbal, Rhiannon Ryall
Magical Guardians - Exploring the Spirit and Nature of Trees, Philip Heselton
Magical History of the Horse, Janet Farrar & Virginia Russell
Magical Lore of Animals, Yvonne Aburrow
Magical Lore of Cats, Marion Davies
Magical Lore of Herbs, Marion Davies

Magick Without Peers, Ariadne Rainbird & David Rankine
Masks of Misrule - Horned God & His Cult in Europe, Nigel Jackson
Medicine For The Coming Age, Lisa Sand MD
Medium Rare - Reminiscences of a Clairvoyant, Muriel Renard
Menopausal Woman on the Run, Jaki da Costa
Mind Massage - 60 Creative Visualisations, Marlene Maundrill
Mirrors of Magic - Evoking the Spirit of the Dewponds, P Heselton
Moon Mysteries, Jan Brodie
Mysteries of the Runes, Michael Howard
Mystic Life of Animals, Ann Walker
New Celtic Oracle The, Nigel Pennick & Nigel Jackson
Oracle of Geomancy, Nigel Pennick
Pagan Feasts - Seasonal Food for the 8 Festivals, Franklin & Phillips
Patchwork of Magic - Living in a Pagan World, Julia Day
Pathworking - A Practical Book of Guided Meditations, Pete Jennings
Personal Power, Anna Franklin
Pickingill Papers - The Origins of Gardnerian Wicca, Bill Liddell
Pillars of Tubal Cain, Nigel Jackson
Places of Pilgrimage and Healing, Adrian Cooper
Practical Divining, Richard Foord
Practical Meditation, Steve Hounsome
Practical Spirituality, Steve Hounsome
Psychic Self Defence - Real Solutions, Jan Brodie
Real Fairies, David Tame
Reality - How It Works & Why It Mostly Doesn't, Rik Dent
Romany Tapestry, Michael Houghton
Runic Astrology, Nigel Pennick
Sacred Animals, Gordon MacLellan
Sacred Celtic Animals, Marion Davies, Ill. Simon Rouse
Sacred Dorset - On the Path of the Dragon, Peter Knight
Sacred Grove - The Mysteries of the Forest, Yvonne Aburrow
Sacred Geometry, Nigel Pennick
Sacred Nature, Ancient Wisdom & Modern Meanings, A Cooper
Sacred Ring - Pagan Origins of British Folk Festivals, M. Howard
Season of Sorcery - On Becoming a Wisewoman, Poppy Palin
Seasonal Magic - Diary of a Village Witch, Paddy Slade
Secret Places of the Goddess, Philip Heselton
Secret Signs & Sigils, Nigel Pennick
Self Enlightenment, Mayan O'Brien
Spirits of the Air, Jaq D Hawkins
Spirits of the Earth, Jaq D Hawkins
Spirits of the Water, Jaq D Hawkins
Spirits of the Fire, Jaq D Hawkins
Spirits of the Aether, Jaq D Hawkins
Stony Gaze, Investigating Celtic Heads John Billingsley
Stumbling Through the Undergrowth , Mark Kirwan-Heyhoe

Subterranean Kingdom, The, revised 2nd ed, Nigel Pennick
Symbols of Ancient Gods, Rhiannon Ryall
Talking to the Earth, Gordon MacLellan
Taming the Wolf - Full Moon Meditations, Steve Hounsome
Teachings of the Wisewomen, Rhiannon Ryall
The Other Kingdoms Speak, Helena Hawley
Tree: Essence of Healing, Simon & Sue Lilly
Tree: Essence, Spirit & Teacher, Simon & Sue Lilly
Through the Veil, Peter Paddon
Torch and the Spear, Patrick Regan
Understanding Chaos Magic, Jaq D Hawkins
Vortex - The End of History, Mary Russell
Warp and Weft - In Search of the I-Ching, William de Fancourt
Warriors at the Edge of Time, Jan Fry
Water Witches, Tony Steele
Way of the Magus, Michael Howard
Weaving a Web of Magic, Rhiannon Ryall
West Country Wicca, Rhiannon Ryall
Wildwitch - The Craft of the Natural Psychic, Poppy Palin
Wildwood King , Philip Kane
Witches of Oz, Matthew & Julia Philips
Wondrous Land - The Faery Faith of Ireland by Dr Kay Mullin
Working With the Merlin, Geoff Hughes
Your Talking Pet, Ann Walker

FREE detailed catalogue and FREE 'Inspiration' magazine
Contact: Capall Bann Publishing, Auton Farm, Milverton, Somerset, TA4 1NE